HOW TO END
MENTAL DEPRESSION

HOW TO END MENTAL DEPRESSION

Carl Weiss

and

Ray Weiss

In consultation with

Dr. Stephen W. Kempster, Psychiatrist

ARCO PUBLISHING COMPANY, INC.
NEW YORK

Published by Arco Publishing Company, Inc.
219 Park Avenue South, New York, N.Y. 10003

Library of Congress Cataloging in Publication Data

Weiss, Carl, 1930–
　　How to end mental depression.

　　Bibliography:　p. 223.
　　Includes index.
　　1.　Depression, Mental.　I.　Weiss, Ray, joint author.
II.　Title.　[DNLM:　1.　Depression—Popular works.
WM170　K29h]

RC537.W34　　　　616.8'52　　　　77–3464
ISBN 0–668–04241–9 (Library Edition)

Printed in the United States of America

Psychopictograms, psychocharts, psychodiagrams,
and all graphics created by Carl Weiss.

THIS EMERGENCY

TREATMENT PROGRAM

IS DEDICATED

TO AMERICA'S UNSUNG HEROES—

THE 70 MILLION DEPRESSIVES,

WHO DEMONSTRATE MATCHLESS COURAGE

BY GOING ON DAY TO DAY

UNTIL THEY END

THEIR MENTAL DEPRESSION

AUTHOR'S NOTE

The names of all patients have been changed to protect their privacy. Where real names are given of people who suffered from mental depression, their cases have already been widely reported to the public by media, prior to the publication of this book.

CONTENTS

PART TWO   /   WHY MENTAL DEPRESSION
                     NEED NOT KILL ITS VIC-
                     TIMS

HOW TO END
MENTAL DEPRESSION

HOW TO
USE
THIS BOOK

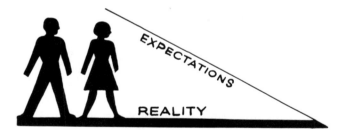

This above all: keep your feet planted on reality as firmly
as possible. Develop expectations that can probably be
made to happen. Don't harbor impossible expectations. In
this way you avoid the danger of too wide a gap between
your expectations and reality. *This overly wide gap is one
of the most serious triggers for a mental depression.* Even
when expectations have excellent chances of succeeding—
always be prepared for its failure. This realistic thinking
defends you from becoming shattered by failed expectations.

Sufferers from a clinical or subclinical mental depression can take heart. Nine out of every ten victims of mental depression emerge from it as mentally alert as they were prior to their developing this mind-dulling condition. The outlook for a complete return to the self that existed prior to the onset of the depression is *very, very* good.

The causes of mental depression and the strategies to help end it are available to you by reading this book.

There is no reason to be ashamed or embarrassed if you are mentally depressed. Remember, President Abraham Lincoln, Prime Minister Winston Churchill, and Senator Thomas Eagleton all suffered from mental depression —*and emerged from it*. All suffered a tremendous deficit in mental productivity during their mental depression. All three were (fortunately for themselves and the world) too realistic to commit suicide while in this condition.

It is now history that when these three emerged from their mental depression they were able to achieve a return to their previous *razor-sharp mentalities*. Their mental productivity is now a matter of historical record.

Read this book carefully. Follow its recommendations. Do the "daily progress reports" at the end of the book, on page 209. Reread this book, because humans tend to forget what they once knew.

By doing this, you are taking realistic steps to help end your present depression—and avoid future depression.

INTRODUCTION

BY
DR. STEPHEN W. KEMPSTER,
PSYCHIATRIST

When asked to work as consultant psychiatrist on this treatment book, I experienced a certain wariness: Can we help end mental depression through a book on its treatment? Over the years, as a practicing psychiatrist, I've had reservations about the value of self-help books. This includes those having to do with mental health, diet, or other medical problems. In addition to treatment of my own patients, most of whom suffer from mental depression, I began to investigate the professional literature on mental depression. Depression is a complicated matter, like life itself—and *must be dealt with*.

Is depression a feeling? Is it a part of the "normal" response of humans to frustrations, to major and minor failures, and is it socially acceptable? We do know that in one form or another it has played and still is playing a large part in the history of man.

To what extent are suicide and depression linked? Psychotherapists Carl Weiss and Ray Weiss, as well as myself, made certain our task here is to offer an ongoing view of the point science has reached today in dealing with this problem. No claims are made except in considering those aspects of depression and suicide which we know something about.

Individual mental depression can be terminated effectively, but it may take from approximately three months to two years. There are many hopeful things we already know that we can state. For example, the very fact that depression is being discussed and written about more frequently is, in itself, a sign of a more scientific approach to it. It is also true that professionals have considerably more tools in their bag than they had twenty years ago.

Such tools consist of increased psychological insights and techniques of coping with mental depression. Additional tools are a variety of active medications which have turned out to be very useful in many psychopathological situations.

Many of these medications, however, have a tranquilizing effect, and, not infrequently, physicians administering them do not monitor their use closely enough. The impact of the medication on the patients over what may be a one- or two-year period must be observed carefully and regularly by the physician. For the first few weeks an antidepressant drug causes the patient to slow down further. It takes a few weeks before the drug takes effect and the patient becomes mentally and physically more active. With patience and perseverance the depression is lifted. It often helps turn the mental depression around within one or two months.

In reviewing the literature, it would appear that there is still a great confusion in the efforts to classify depressions. People persist in describing depression as a rather bad mood, a chronic pessimism, a response to the loss of a near person or a job, etc. It may seem to occur without there being an apparent external cause. It may occur in relation to some serious physical ailment, such as influenza or hepatitis.

Its impairment of a person's functioning can vary greatly. Some depressed people become completely immobilized. Others often become actively suicidal. These people require hospitalization.

On the other hand, the suffering of the vast majority of victims seems to vary from impaired mobility to a severe slowdown, but the depressed persons remain capable of functioning.

This book deals for the most part with that large majority of depressions which do not require hospitalization. These depressions do not involve psychotic symptoms like delusions or hallucinations. In general, if the person involved does not reach a degree of suicidal desperation, he or she usually *recovers*.

In reviewing the literature, it also appears that for recovery some people require six months, some a year and a half, and some up to three years. This includes the natural course of the untreated depression, although professional therapy speeds up the period of recovery considerably.

This practical book constructively addresses itself to certain straightforward tasks. It will help someone to determine whether he is in a depressed state and gives advice on how to act to terminate it. If the person does not experience his depression in precisely mental terms, it may present itself in a variety of physical symptoms, and this not infrequent aspect of depression is considered in this book. It does not claim to offer a perfect solution, or an immediate solution. This is more a program of treatment offering various options which may be useful in curing mental depression. It invites the depressed person to seek other kinds of help—that is, professional help.

Particularly within the last generation or so, mental depression has been very closely linked to guilt, feelings of isolation, and loneliness. It is also true that depression can become a lifestyle: It often becomes habitual as a way of relating to other people, particularly to the family. But whatever mental depressions are (and they are usually enormously complicated) they can gradually evolve into a lifestyle; they can become a way of trying to survive. The depressed person maneuvers other people into assuming responsibilities for him. The depressed person may or may not be able to assume these responsibilities for himself. Such a person may also be suicidal and may talk about it with parents, peers, or whomever. This intimidates those who are concerned about him.

A person who is depressed and suffering agonies needs certain kinds of care. But those close to the depressed person generally find it difficult to understand what is really going on. It's not unlike the story of the boy who cried "wolf." In this kind of situation professional help is required and in this country there are enormous numbers of clinics where such help can be obtained. In the last 17 years, suicide prevention clinics and open telephone or hot-line counselling have become available.

This book adds a new dimension to the many self-help books that I've read. Most of those books tend to make claims which are often unreal. They also tend to be, by implication, critical of the reader if the reader doesn't benefit from reading of the book.

Very often the reader of such a book may be given to expect that he'll suddenly overcome all the problems with which he has lived for a substantial period of his life. In short, there is a kind of seduction in many such books. And if things don't fall into place, it's all *your* fault.

This book makes it reasonably clear that it is not a final answer. However, it does offer help. It also indicates that if the reader does not benefit from the book, there are other real resources available in most communities. These resources can help one not only to define what the problem is but to get the necessary treatment. In other words, the book is practical, rather than ideological.

It indicates in a straightforward way that there is no *dishonor* in involving either family or any other people in an effort to understand and help troubled persons. It also points out that there are limits to which one can go in inviting people to offer help.

The book also ably considers the practical aspects of the findings of the scholars of psychiatry, sociology, and economics.

Human longevity has undergone enormous changes over the last 50 years. In the western world, going back over centuries, man had a life expectancy of 30 years or less. In many parts of the world this kind of life expectancy still exists.

A part of our recent studies includes the depressions associated with the woman in *menopause* and on the "menopause" of the aging male.

Less than a century ago the vast majority of the population never worried about menopause or aging, because people simply didn't live that long. Man, then, was surrounded by a host of diseases, such as tuberculosis, syphilis, and typhoid fever. There were also epidemics of smallpox, bubonic plague, and other diseases which could decimate a community, a city, or a large part of a nation.

We are all aware that sanitaria for the treatment of tuberculosis have disappeared. Polio no longer creates a summer panic. Very recently, an article appeared reporting that smallpox had been all but eliminated.

All of mankind in the past was constantly involved in the struggle for survival. Most of their time was spent hunting for food, seeking shelter from cold, avoiding destructive illness, and waging constant warfare against other groups. An early development in man's recorded history was religion of one kind or another. Although different religions offered different ideals, a common denominator had to do with man's helplessness in coping with the enormity of going on from day to day—and they mainly related to survival.

As religions evolved, many also developed ethical systems. The ten commandments are similar to the ethical systems for other religions. Many aspects of these ethical systems still make a great deal of sense. They tended to pave the way for people to be able to live together and survive.

It is also unfortunately true, however, that man's different religions could serve other kinds of functions. Ethical systems could be employed as a way of controlling one class and keeping it in the service of another.

Religion also imposed a difficult paradox. On the one hand, man was, in effect, sinful; yet it was his personal responsibility not to be so. On the other hand, man was told that he has no authority over his own destiny; that he is in God's hands. So, religion told him that he did not have the power with which to exercise his ethical responsibilities.

This is as if a man who is blind, deaf, and dumb and glued to a wheelchair is assigned the task of being a policeman patrolling a slum area. He is given responsibility while at the same time has no tools with which to carry out the work.

This is an important element in depression. The depressed person is ordered to be as productive as before the depression, yet this is *the* illness that severely reduces productivity. One of the most pervasive components then is the guilt that results. This book attempts to lift some of that guilt off the backs of the depressed.

I have thought about mental depression over the years. I have played with the idea of the ultimate fortune in a Chinese cookie: "It is better to be young, healthy, intelligent, attractive, loved, and rich than to be old, sick, stupid, ugly, disliked, and poor." Unfortunately, many of us are not all that young, intelligent, and so on; and even if all of us *were*, we'd still need *more* than those assets because of the extraordinary ease with which anyone can develop a mental depression.

The fortune cookie saying would have to be expanded a great deal to include other assets. It would have the person incorporate such traits as generosity, social responsibility, societal knowledge, scientific wisdom, expertise, and empathy.

From a variety of levels of professional literature, the press, magazines, radio, and TV, mental depression has emerged as a daily and enormous part of our lives.

Guilt and underestimated shame are very important elements in depression. Some depressions are denied by the sufferer, although painful to him, and are equally denied by those close to him.

Some mental depressions are expressed as a way of blaming and scapegoating others, even though the origin of the mental depression has little to do with those blamed by the depressed person. The *real* causes of such mental depression *can be traced and eliminated*.

There are those depressions labeled "endogenous" (not clearly connected with a cause from the here and now), but some significant loss or failure is usually behind the depression. Some depressions are very severe. They create temporary immobilization and thought disorders. Remember, they are temporary—and should not lead to suicide.

The family plays a role in the development and perpetuation of mental depression. It can also exercise a strong therapeutic influence. This book needs careful study by all members of a depressant's family.

Obviously, important psychotherapy has been developed and is increasingly useful in curing depression. There also are medications which are invaluable when properly monitored; they *do* hasten the recovery of the depressed person.

This book presents a variety of practical measures to the depressed person and his family. It connects constructive everyday possibilities with the professional literature on the treatment of mental depression.

This book avoids the claim of presenting in and of itself a total solution. It urges the use of resources, such as clinics, social agencies, and psychotherapists, to terminate mental depression as rapidly as possible.

We cannot emphasize strongly enough: One should *not* attempt to weather one's mental depression without competent *professional psychotherapy*. Just *one day* of mental depression eliminated by therapy makes the fee and the extra effort worth it all. Professional therapy can check whether you are acting on the treatment offered in this book.

Professional help can terminate a mental depression, because the psychotherapist works to help you *act* on the insights this book documents. Two vital advantages in obtaining help from a psychotherapist are:

1. The psychotherapist explores the patient's strengths and resources that operate even in an extreme mental

depression. These strengths—developed before the onset of the mental depression—must be rediscovered, as the patient is feeling too great a despair to objectively recognize that they are still there.

After the mental depression is terminated, *the abilities you had in the past generally return in full strength.* But in the meantime, using the diminished strengths helps the patient more rapidly to terminate the mental depression.

2. The use of mood-elevating medication can be obtained by the psychotherapist, or an M.D. colleague of those therapists who are not M.D.'s. Talk therapy plus mood-elevation medication make an irresistible combination in terminating nearly all mental depressions. But the medications must be monitored by the psychotherapist to be effective.

This book presents a variety of practical measures to the depressed person and his family. It connects everyday practical activities with the tested strategies to combat the mental depression, as found in professional literature.

Although no footnoted references are included in this Introduction, most of what I've stated has been borrowed from a long list of thoughtful, effective psychotherapists. Thanks to these psychotherapists who preceded us, as well as those who are currently working to terminate mental depression, this book illuminates the problems, and offers some answers to help end mental depression.

New York City,
New York

PART ONE

WHAT YOU MUST KNOW ABOUT MENTAL DEPRESSION

CHAPTER

I

HOW DR. FREUD TERMINATED HIS MENTAL DEPRESSION!

MANY GREAT DISCOVERIES IN HISTORY REQUIRE GENIUSES TO see what they stumbled on. Then it often becomes the *known* common heritage of the world. Unfortunately, Sigmund Freud's discovery that is described in this chapter is *not* generally known to the rest of the world—including psychiatrists and psychologists.

Whenever the name Sigmund Freud comes up in conversation, the same image of Freud invariably arises in most people's minds. He is conceived as a bearded, spectacled, wonder-professor. He is thought of as a brilliant sage who profoundly understood people.

And above all, people believe that Freud knew Socrates' famous injunction, "Know thyself!" And, thinks the average person, if anybody knew himself—that was Dr. Freud!

Not really.

Even at the height of his most brilliant psychological breakthroughs, Freud did not know himself, and he paid dearly for his ignorance . . .

The year was 1895. Freud was thirty-seven years old. Most of his peers, psychiatrists and psychologists had ostracized him. The last straw came when Freud's collaborator, Dr. Josef Bruer, repudiated Freud's new psychology.

Severe stress was no stranger to Dr. Freud.

Freud had a previous history of severe mental depression. Early in his medical career, he had been self-medicating his depressed condition. In 1883, Freud had read with great interest a report by an Austrian army physician, Dr. Theodor Aschenbranft, who had issued cocaine to Bavarian soldiers. The doctor claimed that the soldiers were successfully able to combat fatigue through the use of this drug.

This was precisely what young Dr. Freud was looking for! Chronic fatigue was one of the dreadful symptoms of his mental depression.

Freud was then a poverty stricken neurologist in Vienna. His nervous exhaustion seriously interfered with his daily functioning. He wrote to his fiancée, Martha Bernays, "I'm procuring some cocaine and will try it with cases of heart disease and also of nervous exhaustion."

Freud's official biographer, Dr. Ernest Jones, finds, "Freud tried the effect of a twentieth of a gram [of cocaine] and found it turned the bad mood he was in into cheerfulness giving him the feeling of having dined well, 'so that there is nothing at all one need bother about,' but without robbing him of any energy for exercise or work."

Freud then enthusiastically followed up the first letter to Martha with another: "If it goes well I will write an essay on it [cocaine] and I expect it will find its place in therapeutics by the side of morphium and superior to it.

"I have other hopes and intentions about it. I take very small doses of it regularly against depression and against indigestion. And with brilliant success. . . .

"In short, it is only now that I feel that I am a doctor, since I have helped one patient and hope to help more.

"If things go on in this way we need have no concern about being able to come together and to stay in Vienna."

Young Dr. Freud had even believed that cocaine would solve his penurious state! He had become an innocent drug pusher.

At that period, Freud did his unwitting best to turn whomever he knew into drug addicts! He glowingly advises Martha, "Woe to you, my Princess, when I come. I will kiss you quite red-faced until you are plump.

"And if you are forward, you shall see who is stronger. A gentle little girl who doesn't eat enough or a big wild man *who has cocaine in his body.*

"In my last severe depression I took cocaine again and a small dose lifted me to the heights in a wonderful fashion. I am just now busy collecting the literature for a song of praise."

The mentally depressed Freud erroneously believed that he had accidentally stumbled on the cure for mental depression. He was able to convince other doctors of his erroneous "breakthrough"!

In 1884 Freud had an article published in the very prestigious medical journal, the *Centrallblatt für die gesammte Therapie.* In this "Song of Praise to Cocaine," Freud rhapsodizes over the "gorgeous excitement" that results from cocaine treatment of his mental depression.

Freud praised in the article the effects of small doses of cocaine on his own depression, "[Cocaine gives me] exhilaration, and lasting euphoria. Which in no way differs from the normal euphoria of the healthy person. . . .

"You perceive an increase of self-control and possess more vitality and capacity for work. . . . In other words, you are simply normal. And it is soon hard to believe that you are under the influence of any drug. . . .

"Long intensive mental or physical work is performed without any fatigue. . . . This result is enjoyed without any of the unpleasant after-effects that follow exhilaration brought about by alcohol. . . ."

Freud incorrectly concluded that cocaine is not addictive. He sums it up: "Cocaine is useful for those functional states comprised under the name neurasthenia." (Freud had diagnosed his own depression as neurasthenia.)

Freud was distraught when he discovered the lethal effects cocaine had on his friend Dr. von Fleische-Maxow! Freud, himself, had prescribed cocaine for his friend. Fleische-Maxow had become a cocaine addict—and was using a full gram daily! This cost him $428 for three months—a princely sum in Vienna in 1885. Fleische-Maxow developed a typical cocaine psychosis: "White snakes creeping over and under his skin." Fleische-Maxow lived only a few more years. His mind and body were completely pain-wracked.

Freud hastily abandoned cocaine as a treatment for his patients suffering from mental depression. His own mental depressions came and went. In the 1890's they were particularly disabling.

Two problems particularly troubled Freud at this time. He was unable to meet payment on his bills. And Freud's colleagues and peers in the world of medicine and psychotherapy had rejected his new psychology.

Added to his other problems, Freud's father died—leaving another household to provide for. According to the beliefs of the Victorian 90's, refined women did not work. Freud's mother and sisters depended wholly on his earnings for their support.

Dr. Ernest Jones writes of the problem that was helping to unnerve Freud: "When we reflect that in those years Freud had to support a dozen people, apart from domestic servants, we can understand why finance was a constant anxiety."

Freud makes no reference, in writing, to his earnings in 1896. Small wonder. They were very little. For Freud's views on the importance of the sex drive in humans of every age had effectively isolated him from his colleagues. His fellow professionals' low opinion of his work had cut down his practice to a tiny trickle.

By May, 1896, Freud's consulting room was totally empty. He had had no visits from patients in weeks.

November was just as bad.

The strains of the contemptuous rejection by his colleagues, coupled with the unbearable burden of supporting more than a dozen people, were breaking down Freud's psyche. He described the living hell he found himself in: "I'm in an intellectual paralysis," he rambled in disorganized thought. "Curious state of mind. Which one's consciousness can't apprehend. Twilight thoughts. A veil over one's mind. Scarcely a ray of light here and there."

He was in a period of intense apathy.

As Dr. Jones observes about Freud's very typical mental depression at that time: "Every line that Freud wrote was a torment. And a week later Freud said his inhibition about writing was really pathological."

Freud's admission of a near-total writer's block due to his mental depression is ironical. For Freud was accustomed to write down any matter of importance he was involved in. The most prolific writer on psychological matters, Freud was unable to write because of a psychological block.

All sufferers of a clinical mental depression are in tremendous terror that they may mentally deteriorate further. Freud was no exception. He torturedly writes in the middle of 1897, "I believe I am in a cocoon. And God knows what beast will creep out of it."

It was now January, 1900; Freud's financial situation was more desperate than before. He revealed that he had only managed to get one new case in the past eight months. Numb, he declared, "How I'm going to get through I do not yet know!"

He was to sink even deeper in debt, for in the middle of that year, four patients finished their therapy with him. Freud had no more than a few hours' work daily.

Reeling under these stresses, Freud constantly referred to his "dread of poverty." He wrote that as a youth he had learned what "helpless poverty" is, that he knew what poverty does to its victims. Freud admitted that he was mortally afraid of the effects of poverty. Despite his profound awareness of the destructive effects that poverty had on the psyche, he underestimated poverty's power to help generate in *his own psyche* a clinical mental depression. This underestimation of the effect poverty has on developing a clinical mental depression in *one's own self* is common to most people—including professional psychotherapists.

Dr. Freud confirmed his *theoretical* knowledge of how poverty affects the ability of a person to cope, by declaring, in September, 1891: "You will see that my [work] style will improve and my ideas become more correct when this town gives me plenty to live on."

In 1896, when Dr. Freud's consulting room was empty, so were his thoughts, hopes, and ability to function. But when in December of that year he found work for ten hours daily (earning $40 a day), it was just what the doctor ordered. Freud described the effect this month of earning money had on his behavior, "I'm dead tired, and *mentally fresh!*" Yet this income was soon ended as his patient population was reduced to almost nil.

At this time, Freud had two main goals in life: One was to pay his bills; the other was to discover breakthroughs to cure people's mental illnesses.

Freud enjoyed collecting exquisite and expensive antiques. He also found great pleasure and well-being traveling on vacation and visiting places of antiquity. His lack of money left him unable to take care of both his basic needs and his overriding interests.

Finally, Freud sought the approval and esteem of his colleagues. He knew that his very livelihood significantly depended on the goodwill of his colleagues. His reputation and patient referrals were in the hands of his fellow doctors, and he despised the narrow, jealous antagonism that most of his colleagues displayed toward his discoveries in psychotherapy.

Vienna in the 1890's was pervaded by a haughtiness that affluent patients manifested very clearly by their selection of doctors. Ability in psychotherapy, or in medicine, was not measured by competence—not so far as the patients' choice of a physician was concerned.

What unquestionably determined the reputation and the clientele of the practitioner were the *titles* of the doctors. Well-to-do patients wouldn't dream of engaging a doctor with a *Privatdozent* title—if they could hire a doctor with the coveted title of *Herr Professor*.

Freud's title was only *Privadozent*.

Freud held titles in contempt, yet he could not fail to see the economic necessity of obtaining the *Herr Professor* title.

That Freud despised titles evidenced itself very early in his medical career. This occurred when he was a general practitioner.

At that time he had bought thousands of dollars of electrical machines. These were selected to treat his patients with physical ailments. Freud had bought these expensive machines with the limited money he had at his disposal. He could ill-afford these appliances, but he considered the machines essential in treating rheumatic and arthritic patients. The machines came not only highly recommended by his colleagues, but he had also studied under the much-decorated professor who had manufactured these appliances.

Freud considered that he had to purchase these machines to competently treat his patients. After observing the effect these machines had on his patients, he discovered that they did not do a bit of good for the patients' conditions. Freud scrapped the fraudulent, imposing-looking machines. He bitterly declared he would hereafter disregard honors, titles, and medals that doctors may acquire. His only test for competency of doctor or machine would be: Are they *proven* competent to do the job?

Despite Freud's recognition that the title of *Herr Professor* was vital for his fiscal solvency, he despised its false assumptions. He remained a *Privatdozent* for the untypically long span of twelve years. He wrote resignedly that he was deliberately passed over for young doctors who had better connections in title acquisitions.

Freud's university colleagues' connections were of no avail whatever to him. They conspired, in fact, to blackball him from acquiring the *Herr Professor* title. This enraged Freud, and he decided to make a final break with the university he was affiliated with. Only Professors Kraft-Ebbing,

Nothnagel, and Frankl-Hochwart (in the university) proposed Freud again and again for the position of *Herr Professor.*

These three undaunted and courageous professors decided that, though the Council of the Faculty might blackball Freud, they would go over the Council's head. But then they recognized that the Council of the Faculty is a government institution. The three professors knew the consequences of bypassing the Council's official ratification of Freud's title petition.

The three professors regretfully warned him: "Freud, you know the further difficulties [bypassing the Council will bring]. Perhaps we should achieve nothing more than 'putting you on the carpet.' "

Freud indignantly told the three professors he'd risk making waves.

The three professors pessimistically pressed on. But in spite of these fierce battles by Freud and his handful of supporters, their plan failed miserably. The recommendations for Freud to be granted the title *Herr Professor* were conspiratorily buried by the university and the ministry.

Freud figured he'd done all that was humanly possible to acquire the *essential* title of *Herr Professor.* Despite his envied reputation as a world-renowned neurologist, the title battle seemed hopeless to Freud. *The area of economic survival—an area of importance equal only to breathing—was given up by Freud.*

Freud's frank findings on the role of sexual influences on human behavior made him a leper to polite society. In the Victorian age, he was condemned as an evil and dangerous figure.

At this time, anti-Semitism was still rampant in Austria. It permeated the feelings of those in government circles as well as of the people on the street. For a Jew to achieve the prized *Herr Professor* title was indeed a rarity. The dual barriers of being a Jew as well as *the* discoverer of sex dynamics in the Victorian age convinced Freud that he would never get the *Herr Professor* title.

Shorn of hope, Freud watched the announcements that went out every September of the fortunate few who achieved the *Herr Professor* title. The years 1897, 1898, and 1899 came and went without the title. And in 1900 came what seemed to be the death blow to any last, lingering hopes Freud may have had for the title. For in 1900 all the names but one proposed for the title of *Herr Professor* were ratified by the minister. The only one excluded from this list was Sigmund Freud.

Freud was crushed. He let four years pass. He made no further fight in this key area of his economic survival. But four years of relentless piling up of debts were too painful to endure passively.

Freud began to fight again. A former professor of Freud's was high in the ministry's counsel. Hat in hand, Freud asked Professor Exner to help him get that essential piece of paper bestowing the *Herr Professor* title. Professor Exner behaved in his own characteristic manner to his former star pupil. Freud revealed what then took place to his confidant, Dr. Wilhelm Fliess:

"So I decided to break with my strict principles and take some practical steps as other human beings do. One has to seek one's salvation somewhere, and I chose the title of Professor to be my savior.

"For four long years I hadn't offered a word to further it. Now I decided to call on my old teacher, Exner. He was as unpleasant as possible, almost rude, refused to disclose any reasons for my having been ignored, and generally assumed the airs of the high official.

"Only after I provoked him with a few sarcastic remarks about the goings-on of those in high places did he drop some obscure hints about personal influences that were prejudicing His Excellency against me. He advised me to seek some counterinfluence.

"I was in the position to tell him that I would approach my old friend and former patient, the wife of *Hofrat* Gomperz.

"This seemed to impress him. Frau Elise was most amiable and took an immediate interest.

"She called on the Minister in question and in answer to her request was greeted by a face of astonishment, 'A doctor strove for four years to receive the title of *Herr Professor*? And who may that be?' "

When Frau Gomperz disclosed to Freud the minister's answer, Freud acted hardly surprised. Wryly, Freud revealed to Frau Gomperz that "the old fox" enjoyed pretending his memory of Freud was dim. Yet the same minister, Freud recalled, eyed him sharply when Freud had presented himself to him four years ago. The minister instantly had observed, "Dr. Freud, I've heard excellent things about you!"

The battle continued. Freud was addressing his former patient and pleader in court as "Your Highness." He, indeed, hardly underestimated the service she was performing for his survival. He used every weapon to survive. He now was calling Frau Gomperz "Dear Protectix." And he meant it!

All information that might help Frau Gomperz's campaign to get Freud his title was brought to her by him. Expert though she had now become regarding Freud's eligibility for the title of *Herr Professor*, the minister was more adroit. He consistently and successfully avoided the Gomperzes. They were personae non gratis.

It was the final blow. Freud was totally disheartened. He described his abject dependency on "business [which is nearly non-existent] on which my mood invariably depends."

He had finally stumbled on the chief cause of most mental depression. As his earnings came to a near-halt, Freud recognized this as the main cause of his severe mental depressions. He declared: "Work and earnings are identical to me, so that I've become fully carcinoma [cancerous]!"

As his little work and pitiful earnings continued, Freud mourned: "Today I have to go to the theatre. It is ridiculous. As if anyone could transplant anything to a carcinoma. Nothing else could stick to it. And my *existence is from now on* that of neoplastic [cancer]!"

His failure to provide a living for his family had enslaved Freud's entire mentality. He was so emotionally numb, he could barely protest how cruel life was. Desperate, he was ready to give up his private psychoanalytic practice.

Freud frantically tried to get a job at a sanitarium for the slow summer months. He had to raise some money for food, clothing, and shelter. He failed to find a job. Then, a random act occurred which changed Sigmund Freud's life. In turn, it changed the world of psychotherapy.

From out of the blue—a new combatant entered the lists on Freud's side. Yet another patient of Freud's joined the battle to obtain the title of *Herr Professor* for Freud. Her name was Frau Marie Feistel, the wife of a diplomat.

She learned about the withheld title and she recognized some of its dire consequences. She surveyed the debacle resulting from the failure of the renowned professors, and Freud himself, to overthrow the Austrian anti-Semitic and Victorian state policies. But to save her depressed psychotherapist, she would not bow to the apparently irreversible defeat. Besides, she had learned that another of Dr. Freud's patients had tried to aid his desperate situation. Frau Marie Ferstel had decided that she would not take second place to Frau Elise Gomperz. She, Frau Ferstel, would save her beloved psychoanalyst.

Freud described her actions: "Frau Ferstel refused to rest until she had made the minister's acquaintance at a party.

"She managed to ingratiate herself with him.

"And, via a mutual lady friend, made him *promise* to confer a professorship on the doctor who had cured her (but who himself was ill with a mental depression)."

Freud now learned of the real determination and astuteness of Frau Ferstel. He says, greatly impressed: "But [Frau Ferstel] was well enough informed to know that a promise from him [the minister] was as good as *none*."

It is believed that every person has a price that will close a deal. Cannily, Frau Ferstel established the minister's price. She rejected the loser's strategy of winning the title for Freud on his merits *alone* (as a neurologist).

The minister was aflame, she soon learned, to acquire a modern painting by Arnold Böcklin: "A Castle in Ruins." This painting, if it could be gotten, would be the highlight at the opening of the newly established Vienna Modern Gallery.

As of this date, the minister had failed miserably in persuading the painting's owner to part with it. The owner prized the painting far beyond any money or honors offered in exchange for it. Neither the minister, nor the Modern Gallery of Vienna made any inroads in obtaining the longed-for painting.

The owner of this Böcklin was Frau Ernestine Thorsch—*the aunt of Frau Ferstel*!

Every wile was used by Frau Ferstel to separate the painting from her old aunt. At the end of three months, Aunt Thorsch succumbed to her niece's supplications and blandishments.

That night, at Frau Ferstel's dinner party, the minister graciously made a formal statement. He informed the ecstatic hostess and the assembled guests that, prior to informing the press, he wanted them to be the first to know of a special announcement of importance. He told them he had sent the documents to the Emperor Franz Josef granting the title of *Herr Professor* to the world-renowned Austrian neurologist, Dr. Sigmund Freud.

Early the next day, Frau Ferstel burst into Dr. Freud's office, radiant. In her hand she victoriously brandished a pneumatic-tube-propelled letter.

She cried exultantly, *"Ich hab's gemacht!* (I did it!)" The long elusive passport for Freud's economic survival had at last been obtained! Freud had labored well with his patient Frau Ferstel. He had helped fashion a mind that excelled his own and his colleague professors' when it came down to the skin game!

The *Weiner Zeitung*, Vienna's leading newspaper, had not yet completed printing the news on Dr. Freud's admittance into the privileged caste with the *Herr Professor* title. Yet as the joyful bemused Freud sat in his study, congratulations and flowers were pouring in. Word of mouth had spread the unlikely news throughout Vienna!

Bewildered, Freud resorted to wit. He struck a pose of a conquering hero and joked, to cover his vast emotional relief, "Public enthusiasm is immense!

"The role of sexuality has suddenly been realized by His Majesty!

"The importance of dreams confirmed by the Council of Ministers!

"The necessity of treating hysteria by psychoanalytic theory is accepted in Parliament by a two-thirds majority!"

The *Herr Professor* title had opened the doors to success—rather than Freud's great, historical contributions to psychology!

This Alice-in-Wonderland turn of events reaped immense rewards. Freud's distant acquaintances and colleagues who had *formerly* detoured to the other side of the street on catching sight of him, *now* went out of their way to shake the great man's hand. Even from a distance, they would bow at sighting him.

Freud's neighbor's children had formerly been warned by their parents to avoid associating with his children. Now they were instructed to seek out the Freud children and play with them, whenever the opportunity presented itself.

In school, where Freud's children had been ostracized, envious classmates now clustered around them.

Freud was summoned to be personally presented to the Emperor to receive his honored title. It was obligatory that Dr. Freud wear his military service medal.

Freud hadn't the slightest interest in the military. Honorably discharged as a military doctor, he had promptly lost his medal. In this "emergency" his friend Herzig loaned him *his* medal. He cautioned Freud to be ready when the eagle-eyed Emperor caught sight of him entering the Royal Audience Chamber. He should expect the Emperor to roar, "Herr Professor Freud, isn't that Herzig's medal?"

Thereafter, Herr Professor Freud was flooded with eager patients!

Courageously, Freud admitted that he himself had not known how to assure his own survival. "In the whole story there is one person who has proved himself to be an ass— that is me," he said.

"If I had taken these steps [reached the minister where he was reachable] three years ago I would have been appointed three years earlier [to *Herr Professor*], and spared myself a great deal."

Freud's office door was never closed again. Throngs of patients clamored to fit into his now ever-busy schedule. Other psychotherapists and the general public now bought Freud's published work by the millions. Royalties and honors poured in endlessly *after* his fiscal base had been made secure by obtaining the elusive title of *Herr Professor*. For Freud, these two words spelled the termination of his severe clinical mental depression!

In the actual life experience of Dr. Freud, the creator of the Reality Principle, we learn of the nearly inevitable mental depression that develops after a long period of failing to meet bills. Mental depression is also caused by stresses other than financial, but very few people with severe, long-term, financial stress can avoid a clinical mental depression. Sigmund Freud emphatically was *not* among the rare few who escaped it.

Most of the time, mental depressions are caused by a combination of more than one serious stress. As a result, removal of the financial pressure alone may not be sufficient to terminate all mental depressions, for *the three most important factors in human lives are*:

1. the quality of the sexual or marital relationship;
2. the occupation one earns a living from; and
3. the friends and social life one engages in.

Freud had successfully met his sexual needs. His passionate love for Martha ranks with the great love affairs. In addition to the painstaking research Freud had engaged in, his personal experience prompted him to affirm that "Nothing in life is as pleasurable as the sexual act." So vital was sex revealed to Freud through his research, that one of his greatest accomplishments was to remove it from the supposed realm of pleasure and luxury and to put it in its proper place—a necessity for survival.

Freud's active social life, among close friends, has equally set an enviable historical record. Courageous professional colleagues, who dared the wrath of official circles, stood by Freud—even against the Austrian monarch himself! To socialize with Freud was a heady stimulus. His company was sought after by Europe's finest minds. And this was before the world recognized his genius.

But his financial impoverishment presented an entirely different picture. It had seemed to Freud to be insurmountable. His inability to earn enough to keep up with his family's growing needs caused Freud desperately to utilize every spare moment to search for income. His powerful drive to do psychological research had to be frustrated as he made frantic efforts to earn money.

In Freud's case, he had come to working terms with his other key stresses, but his overwhelming financial stresses were his undoing. His inability to pay his bills and to maintain his family and himself, triggered in him a constant feeling of hopelessness. It had developed into a hopelessness related to every act and every situation he was in.

However, when Dr. Freud's financial burden was lifted, his mental depression lifted also. His case was one where money was the cure that was needed.

Freud had his mental depression terminated thanks to the able efforts of his patient. But in his next thirty-seven years, he fruitfully and brilliantly discovered methods to help end mental depression.

No effective book on mental depression treatment can be complete unless it includes Freud's important discoveries about mental depression.

II

SELF-EXAMINATION TEST TO DETERMINE IF YOU HAVE A CLINICAL OR SUBCLINICAL MENTAL DEPRESSION

Are You One of the Seventy Million People Walking Around with a Mental Depression— and Don't Know It?

BEFORE AN ILLNESS CAN BE HEALED, IT MUST BE IDENTI-fied. Most untreated victims of a mental depression are un-aware of *what* is devastating their personalities. Frequently, these victims unwittingly mask their mental depression by "self medicating" themselves with excessive liquor and drugs.

Of a population of over two hundred million Ameri-cans, 70,000,000 are suffering from mental depression. Some period in their lives may be spent in a mental institu-tion. The reason only one in every ten is institutionalized is that there is not a sufficient number of beds for our seri-ously mentally depressed. Nearly all mentally ill patients suffer mental depression as well.

Therapists are able to treat patients once they have removed the mystery regarding the identity of their ailment. The following test helps determine whether the patient is suffering from a mental depression:

SELF-EXAMINATION TEST TO DETERMINE WHETHER YOU MAY HAVE A CLINICAL OR SUBCLINICAL MENTAL DEPRESSION

	YES	NO	
(1)	☐	☐	I have virtually no appetite.
(2)	☐	☐	I feel everything is hopeless.
(3)	☐	☐	I suffer from feelings of great inferiority.
(4)	☐	☐	I think of suicide as the easiest way out.
(5)	☐	☐	I have virtually no sex drive.
(6)	☐	☐	It takes me a very long time to manage to fall asleep.
(7)	☐	☐	I regularly awaken in the middle of my sleep.
(8)	☐	☐	I can't fall asleep again, after I awaken in the middle of my sleep.
(9)	☐	☐	I constantly feel very tired.
(10)	☐	☐	I can't seem to end my tiredness with a refreshing night's sleep.
(11)	☐	☐	My memory is not what it used to be.
(12)	☐	☐	My attention span is very poor.
(13)	☐	☐	My legs, arms, shoulders, and other parts of my body feel uncoordinated to me.
(14)	☐	☐	What I formerly did with great ease, I now find requires great effort to do.
(15)	☐	☐	I'm much slower now in nearly everything I do.

	YES	NO	
(16)	☐	☐	I feel constant stress and anxiety.
(17)	☐	☐	I find that I smile and laugh less than before.
(18)	☐	☐	I now find it much more difficult to understand people.
(19)	☐	☐	I fear my mind is becoming retarded.
(20)	☐	☐	I'm afraid that people will think I'm behaving in a peculiar way.
(21)	☐	☐	I feel that life is passing me by.
(22)	☐	☐	I feel that I'm no longer an adequate person.
(23)	☐	☐	I don't like being me.
(24)	☐	☐	I fear I'm losing touch with reality.
(25)	☐	☐	I feel that I'm living in a nightmare.
(26)	☐	☐	I feel lonely, even when I'm surrounded by people I know.
(27)	☐	☐	I don't like to be with people because I'm afraid they will reject me.
(28)	☐	☐	I feel uncomfortable, even with friends.
(29)	☐	☐	I'm afraid to meet new people.
(30)	☐	☐	I'm unable to make new friends.
(31)	☐	☐	I can't think of new ideas.
(32)	☐	☐	I find it extremely hard to make conversation.
(33)	☐	☐	It's now hard for me to make decisions.
(34)	☐	☐	I fear I'm going to become a dependent person.
(35)	☐	☐	I fear I'm going to become a helpless person.

IMPORTANT!

A clinical or subclinical depression is like pneumonia. And just like pneumonia, mental depression for most people, is a *temporary* illness. The quickest way to terminate this agonizing condition is to obtain competent therapeutic treatment. This ensures a considerably quicker recovery; but even with no treatment, *nine out of ten sufferers will always recover*! This recovery is usually *complete*: all former mental skills and quickness returns.

HOW TO SCORE THE TEST:

An *emphatic* "YES" answer to 23 of the 35 questions on the test above indicates one is probably suffering from a *clinical* mental depression.

A *moderate* "YES" answer to 23 questions indicates one may be suffering from a *subclinical* mental depression.

If 23 of the 35 questions on this test are answered by "YES" then you would be well advised to seek professional help.

In addition to the necessity of the depressive's knowing what his illness is in order to terminate it, it is useful to know if significant others (parents, spouse, sibling, child, friends, etc.) are clinically mentally depressed. The above questionnaire applies to this network of significant others, as well as the depressed sufferer. If any in this network are similarly mentally depressed, they also require psychotherapy. The sooner they terminate their depression, the sooner will the depressed sufferer overcome his depression.

CHAPTER

III

SUICIDE
NEED NOT OCCUR
DUE TO
MENTAL DEPRESSION

WHEN THE MENTAL DEPRESSION DIAGNOSIS IS DEFINITELY established, one should know this comforting fact: *Psychotherapists have discovered that the surest, fullest recovery from any category of mental illness is recovery from mental depression.* Yet mental depression is a very dangerous condition—because nearly 700,000 people die from it yearly, through totally unnecessary suicide.

But *not one single suicide need occur due to mental depression*! We can't overemphasize this reassuring truth about mental depression: *Nine out of ten people suffering from mental depression will terminate it*!

They will end their condition of depression in less than one or two years. Their recovery to their former self will be complete. No debilitating signs of mental depression will remain with these former sufferers from this condition.

Below are the facts regarding obsessive suicide thoughts as a symptom, as well as a consideration of the danger of their being carried out, during mental depression:

"Depression, one of the major health problems of today, is *the most common* psychiatric disorder treated in office practice

58

and outpatients' clinics. The study of depression is important, not only because of the human misery it causes, but because its byproduct, suicide, *is a leading cause of death* in certain age groups."

AARON T. BECK, M.D., PSYCHIATRIST.
American Handbook of Psychiatry.

* * *

"Fourteen percent diagnosed as depressives committed suicide."

Study by Drs. A. Pederson, D. Barry, and
—H. M. BABAGIAN, *Epidemiological*
Considerations of Psychotic Depressions.

* * *

"The suicide rate among former psychiatric patients in a veterans hospital in Texas is twenty-five times the expected rate."

Study by Dr. A. D. Pokorny, *Suicide Rates*
in Various Psychiatric Disorders.

* * *

"It was found that the suicide rate for mental depressives is thirty-six times higher than that committed by the general public."

Study by Drs. A. Temoche, T. F. Pugh, and
B. MacMahon, *Suicide rates among Current*
and Former Mental Institution Patients.

* * *

Even the most brilliant people can become mentally depressed. Our society can't afford the annual suicides of thousands of its brilliant members—such as the Drs. Stewart and Cyril C. Marcus. Their condition of mental depression could have been terminated under proper treatment:

2 Gynecologists Called
Despondent by Colleague

The mysterious deaths of the Marcus brothers, gynecologists and identical twins whose bodies were found in their York Avenue apartment on Thursday, may have been the result of *suicidal despondency* after each had suffered an *emotional breakdown*, a doctor close to them said yesterday.

Medical colleagues and former patients described the two brothers as "brilliant men." Dr. Gideon Panter, a gynecologist, said the textbook the brothers edited on obstetrics and gynecology was "one of the major textbooks" in the field.

Robert H. Abel, a writer whose wife, Carol, was treated through two difficult pregnancies by Stewart Marcus, said, "We owe our children to Dr. Marcus."

Neighbors on their floor of the building, which is known as Sutton Terrace, said the two brothers seldom talked to anyone. *

Even the most powerful people can become mentally depressed. Secretary of the Interior Stanley K. Hathaway, suffering from a clinical depression, need no more have resigned from his job than did Senator Thomas F. Eagleton during his mental depression. (A key symptom of mental depression is the almost unshakeable belief by its sufferers that they will never terminate their present state of mental helplessness. Instead, they *erroneously* believe that their former mental skills and other abilities will never fully return.)

Regardless of their positions in society, the vast numbers of mentally depressed can utilize emergency treatment.

---

* From *The New York Times*, July 21, 1975.

Able psychotherapeutic treatment can prevent the mental depressive from overthrowing a lifetime of work by the rash decision, "I'll never be as good again."

Although Secretary Hathaway did resign from his job, he did *not* commit suicide, but rather sought treatment:

Hathaway Suffers
From 'Depression'

Secretary of the Interior Stanley K. Hathaway said in a hospital statement today that he was suffering from "moderate depression" brought on by overwork.

Mr. Hathaway was undergoing psychiatric treatment as a part of the medical treatment at nearby Bethesda (Md.) Naval Hospital.

The 51-year-old former Governor of Wyoming said nothing in his three-paragraph late afternoon statement about resigning. . . .

Want to Be Careful

"Nobody is quite sure which way it's going to go," the official said, adding that *Mr. Hathaway "does feel he wants to resign but everybody wants to be very careful before a final decision is made."*

In his public statement, Mr. Hathaway said that since he had decided to enter the Naval Medical Center, at nearby Bethesda, Md., at about 4:30 P.M. last Tuesday—a decision not announced by the Interior Department until last Thursday in response to newsmen's questions *that described him as "exhausted" and suffering from loss of weight*—his doctors had advised him that "he is progressing well and is in satisfactory condition."

His statement today said:

"Mr. Hathaway said he had himself decided that he required treatment and notified President Ford on July 15. The

White House physician, Rear Adm. William M. Makash, recommended that the Secretary go to the Bethesda Hospital for observation and treatment. He was admitted at approximately 4:30 P.M. July 15.

One visitor to his tower 10 suite at the hospital, however, said that over the weekend, *Mr. Hathaway had felt "terribly weak" and had remained slumped in a chair.**

Innumerable case histories prove that many brilliant people are among the present 70 million mentally depressed victims in the nation. Regardless of possessing a brilliant or an average mind, sixty-three million of these depressed will fully recover their mental abilities. What a tragic mistake for mentally depressed people to commit suicide when 9 out of 10 times their mental depression can be totally terminated!

======

* From *The New York Times*, July 22, 1975.

CHAPTER
IV

THE *MOST* IMPORTANT FACT OF LIFE

YEARS AGO, ONE OF OUR CLINICAL PSYCHIATRY PROFESSORS asked his class, "What is the most important fact of life?"

One resident psychiatrist answered, "Love."

"That's not the answer," said the professor.

"Is it equality?" ventured a second resident psychiatrist.

"No, that's not it either," the professor replied.

"Peace?" ventured another resident psychiatrist. (This was during an era of war.)

"No." The professor held up his hand to signal no more answers.

He answered his own question, solemnly and emphatically, "Survival!"

He was right. Love is essential, equality is essential, peace is essential—but only *survival* makes all this possible!

In the *Wisdom of the Fathers*, the ancient collection of Hebrew sages reveal, "If *I* am not for myself, *who* will be?"

True. Life is too difficult for this truth to be ignored or merely paid lip service to.

The sages also added, "But if I don't concern myself about the survival of others, *what* am I?"

After one makes sure of one's own survival, then, and only then, does one help others to survive. Here are two acts that can't be underestimated. But they must be attended to in the proper order. First comes *you*, then others. And if you don't help yourself first, you will not be able to help others effectively.

It is vital to recognize that you can help others survive while you're engaged in the battle to survive. Helping others to survive helps you to survive. For it relieves you of feelings of guilt that you are a bad or worthless person. No one who helps others is likely to experience conscience pangs or deep, disturbing guilt; and helping others makes one feel less helpless.

A psychologist friend, Robert Latham, had suffered a severe stroke. This occurred years before he became a psychologist. His recovery from the disabling effects of the stroke was very slow. He found he was unable to think clearly, as he had been able to in the past. He discovered his creativity, his speech, his very memory had all gone downhill.

He felt very depressed, mentally retarded, and helpless.

Mr. Latham figured out a remedy.

He volunteered to work in a school for the mentally retarded. He tutored the youngsters. The psychiatrist in charge of the program appreciated the effort, for here was a somewhat mentally impaired victim of a stroke helping the mentally retarded develop their mental capacities!

The stroke victim worked with the mentally retarded for a year. By that time he had fully recovered his previous mental resourcefulness. His articulate, easy speech and vast vocabulary had fully returned.

In his efforts to help the more mentally disabled, Mr. Latham had regained his former mental capacity. As people help other people in distress, their mental image of themselves as helpless, inadequate, or inferior becomes difficult to maintain. The more they aid others, the more adequate and self-confident they become.

Mr. Latham was fortunate. He knew what type of activity he should engage in to pull himself out of his post-stroke mental depression.

Most depressed persons may require help in selecting the kinds of activity they might best engage in to recover their self-esteem and self-confidence.

An intelligent spouse, friend, or, preferably, psychotherapist can be of great value in making such judgments. The depressive's mind is often tainted or distorted by his illness and he finds his judgment and decision-making capacities impaired. This is inherent in the depressive illness.

Despite the value to one's self-image of cooperating with others, many believe that "good guys finish last." How necessary is it to constantly step on others' necks in order to survive?

The benefits of cooperation and helping those weaker than yourself are self-evident, and the price for ruthless treatment of others may be the addition of significant causes for a clinical mental depression.

This is a complicated area, for being too "cooperative" and making too many compromises in areas of one's real self-interests can also be injurious. By using a submissive, self-diminishing approach to *all* encounters, *one can prolong a depression.*

CHAPTER

V

STRATEGIES
FOR
MENTAL SURVIVAL

WHEN THE AUTHORS WERE RESEARCHING A BOOK ON LIFE in prisons, a "survivalist" surfaced. Warden John Case* is this rare, healthy type. He showed this trait when he spoke to us of his ever-present "P.M.B."

After we queried what that meant, he said, his eyes twinkling, "Why, that means 'protect my back!' Do you know how much good I can do for my inmates if I don't protect my back? Why, I'd get shot down by my enemies so fast, it'd make your head spin!"

Unfortunately, most depressives rarely practice "P.M.B." They tend to neglect their financial security—though they may pay lip service to its necessity. They neglect eating proper amounts of the right kind of food. They overlook the required amounts of sleep and rest. This

---

* Warden John Case is a giant of a man. An ex-marine major, he is built as powerfully as the ancient three-feet-thick stone walls of his Bucks County Prison in Pennsylvania. Warden Case uses his "protect my back" power, as he says "to salvage my inmates—not to junk them." (From *Terror in the Prisons* by Carl Weiss and David James Friar, Bobbs-Merrill, New York, 1975. Ray Weiss researched the effect prisons have on the psyches of their inmates.)

makes them prey to illness and constant physical and mental fatigue. They are now prone to becoming clinically mentally depressed.

They neglect *working at* sufficient relaxing pastimes, and end up in a regular state of anxiety, worry, stress, strain, and irritability. They may love their fellow humans, but the above behavior shows little love for *themselves.*

To love oneself does not mean it is impossible to love others. Two devastating symptoms felt in a depression are:

— belief that one is selfish;
— belief one is uncaring of others.

The person suffering from mental depression will hasten its departure by loving his or her fellow humans. This is a prescription which will lead to the depression's termination. It also is a defense against developing a mental depression condition.

The psychotherapist's job is working with people with serious problems; foremost among these are *money* problems. We've met every type of patient wrestling with every imaginable financial burden. We've observed them as individuals, as groups, members of unions, communes, and manufacturing associations.

We've never met, treated, or heard of anybody who had figured out how to get by without money (by labor or inheritance) for food, clothing, shelter, medical care, educational needs, recreational needs, and miscellaneous expenses.

Sooner or later, everyone comes to the inescapable conclusion that money is as indispensable as oxygen. Neither oxygen nor money guarantee happiness, yet both are essential to survival.

Money = the concentrated sweat of labor (or inheritance) = products and services necessary for survival.

That's why money is the essential force that makes the world go round, at least at this time in history.

It is possible that in the very far future our money system may be more humane. At present, neither the West nor the East have come up with a system that makes the "money = labor" formula obsolete.

Whenever we live beyond our means, we pay for the long period of overspending with the massive strain on our nervous system. For the overspender is interfering with the economic systems that presently run the world. This is a cruel fact—and real.*

The Bible echoes this terrible reality in grim fashion, "By the sweat of your brow shall you eat bread!"

This is the law of life that still pertains today. "Corporeal punishment," far beyond the loanshark's limb breaking, always results when we ignore this law.

This "punishment" is meted out to many. It is possibly the worst "punishment" ever devised. Words can never adequately describe the agony it inflicts on its victims.

No body language can possibly show its pain, regardless of the most frightful grimaces and body contortions. Never can the agony and the anguish be shown in all its horror.

No painter can possibly picture it. No actor can simulate this terrible "punishment." No poet, regardless of the scope of sensitivity he or she possesses, can transmit the infinite depth of hurt this "punishment" inflicts.

---

* National governments are primarily *mercantile* enterprises. Allegiance to ethical behavior between and among countries is contingent on *secure financial relationships*."—Irwin Berger, Professor of English at the Bronx Community College, New York.

If every last torture conceived by man were to be applied to the most vulnerable of victims, it would pale compared to the "punishment" we speak of. If every possible psychological technique of pain were applied, it would equal only a faint vestige of the unspeakable "punishment" visited on its sufferers.

This "punishment" is so excruciatingly painful, that some victims act out the final role of the totally desperate—suicide!

This "punishment" has a name—*subclinical* or *clinical mental depression.*

*   *   *

We must emphasize a second law of survival behavior: *Some tactics that work at one time, may not automatically work later in one's life.*

For example, what may work well for an infant of six months can be very destructive to a child of ten years. When a six-month-old infant requires food, diaper change, or love, he wails for it. If a ten-year-old were to weep for food, apparel, and love, he'd be nearly ten years behind in his acquiring tactics. His old tactics not only wouldn't work, they would be destructive to achieving the goals of a ten-year-old.

In this prescribed treatment you're reading, you may find some contradictions present. It's part of life itself—contradictions do occur. This is because life is very complex, and in a state of constant change. That makes it impossible invariably to follow a "line," or automatic directives.

There are times to advance, and times to retreat.

There are times to *expose oneself to the dangers of possible stress.* There are instances when it's worth taking risks. Developing a love relationship involves this type of worthwhile risk-taking. If the relationship works, one has a vital need met. If it fails, one may be hurt. Under certain circumstances, a *calculated risk* is worth taking.

There are other times when self-protective action is called for, rather than exposing oneself to risks. If a *potential* love object is, for example, a drug addict, then self-protection calls for not risking developing this relationship.

As Gilbert and Sullivan wisely put it, "A paradox, a paradox, a most ingenious paradox!" One must be alert to a sudden need for changes in tactics for the desired result.

CHAPTER
VI

**MENTAL SURVIVAL
IS HELPED
BY A *NETWORK OF
SIGNIFICANT OTHERS***

THE POSSESSION OF A NETWORK OF SIGNIFICANT OTHER people is most important to mental health. Barbra Streisand appealingly and longingly sang of this law of survival: "People need people."

The depressed sufferer needs a network of significant others who he can use. He can't afford to cut himself off from this network. If he *has* cut himself off, he must take steps to revitalize the network. In developing, maintaining, and using this network, professional help by the psychotherapist may be required.

Many so-called spontaneous recoveries may result from the successful intervention of this network. Where this network of significant others is being used well, it may sometimes eliminate the need for professional help.

Very often, however, the victims of depression have isolated themselves. They resist this intervention of their network for various reasons, including false shame. But the depressed sufferer will accept the psychotherapist's aid in enlisting the network to help terminate the depression. Here the psychotherapist may encourage the depressed person to join a therapy group, a club, or an activity that necessitates relating to people. Even a modest beginning is an important start in terminating the depression. *Self-isolating moves by the depressives rarely, if ever, reduce depression.*

The psychotherapist's suggestions for self-help by the depressives may require some help from others. This may vary from friendly encouragement for the depressive to engage in specific social activities to firm prodding by the family and the network.

Hopefully, the depressive will be amenable to friendly, sympathetic encouragement. But if bitter medicine (firm prodding) is indicated, the depressive should try it—he won't like it, but the results may please him.

The depressed person is like a growing child. He has a fluctuating capacity to exercise good judgment, make decisions, and assume responsibility.

When the depressive develops a realistic recognition of the difficulties related to his depression, his sense of self-respect and dignity will not be continually damaged. He will more effectively get on with living, while overcoming his depressed state.

CHAPTER

VII

THE EFFECTS
ONE'S JOB
HAS ON
MENTAL DEPRESSION

DR. FREUD SAW PEOPLE AS "ICEBERGS." HE EXPLAINED that just as only the tip of the iceberg is seen, so only are 10 percent of people's thoughts conscious:

THE HUMAN THINKING PROCESS:

10% IS **CONSCIOUS** THINKING

90% IS **UNCONSCIOUS** THINKING

We find this true, and add this extra dimension to the human thinking process:

THE HUMAN THINKING PROCESS:

10% OF PEOPLE'S THINKING IS INFLUENCED BY THEIR LOOKS, HEALTH, PERSONALITY (SENSE OF HUMOR, CHARM, ATTITUDES), ETC.

90% OF PEOPLE'S THINKING IS INFLUENCED BY THEIR JOBS OR ROLES IN LIFE

You are mainly your *job*. Your schedule on your job, for the most part, keeps you structured. It is the cement that keeps you from coming apart. Dr. Hyman Weiner of Columbia University uncovered, with the authors, case histories that prove the essential necessity for mental stability for most people is to work at a job—particularly if that person is mentally depressed. The job is among the strongest tools for the depressed person to maintain successful ties with family, friends, and responsibilities.

Above all, the job is an expression of *resistance* that still lives in depressed persons. As long as depressed persons use every device in their power to *assert* themselves, they are functioning. Assertion is not aggression. Assertion is the refusal by an organism to be ploughed under by others or by adverse events.

Ms. Ann Hannes is a certified clinical counselor who is outstanding in helping others retain or get jobs. She was trained at the graduate school of C. W. Post Center of Long Island University. She explains the vital nature of her work: "What can be done to help the unemployed professional or executive of any age who is beginning to feel lost?

"How about the special problems of the unemployed in his middle years? What about the college graduate who is demoralized at not finding a job after spending years, effort, and money in preparing for a career?

"This brings to mind a Ph.D. who broke down and cried when applying for a job as a waitress after looking for a job in her field for months. Unemployment's emotional impact on each individual has been inadequately dealt with.

"The statistics of the millions who are unemployed represent people. People trying to support their families. Young people as professionals seeking their first positions.

"Some unemployed people have been searching for work too often. They now go at it half-heartedly.

"Another problem occurs when the family bread-winner loses his job or takes a pay cut. His wife or teenage children may be forced to go out to seek work.

"These events frequently affect all the members of the family with feelings of inadequacy and the downgrading of the self-image of the breadwinner.

"The spouse, if she is fortunate enough to find employment, frequently finds that her life is submerged in the pressures of her job as well as the domestic upsets that drain her energy, absorb her time, and cause anxiety.

"The teenage children who were forced out to work have to give up an opportunity for education. There follows a feeling of alienation and bitterness.

"Many middle-class families, unaccustomed to unemployment and its privations, are thrown into crises. They range from a husband running away, to the stresses leading to consideration of divorce.

"Change of roles with the woman as the breadwinner has traumatic effect on both spouses and on the children.

"Even *temporary* unemployment has social, interpersonal, and psychological impact on the whole family. There is an urgent need to help people deal with this transitional period."

Since lack of money is such a powerful stress trigger to depressed people, Ms. Hannes declares: "Money is not an issue with me. I'm interested in helping the human condition. That's what I'm essentially concerned with. I'm trained. I have the time. Why not?"

Ms. Hannes offers her counselling service to deal with unemployment free of charge.

Associate professor of psychiatry at Yale, Dr. James P. Comer, confirms Ms. Hannes' diagnosis of the psychological havoc unemployment plays on the entire family. He discloses: "What is the effect of unemployment on parent and child relationships?

"Our most accepted principles of child development tell us that preparation for adulthood does not begin with the 18-year-old, the 10-year-old, not even entirely with the infant.

"It begins with the parents, their hopes, plans, and sense of belonging in the community and society. It begins in their sense of *personal adequacy* and specific child-rearing skills.

"Nothing speaks louder to their sense of belonging and adequacy, nothing shapes their hopes and dreams and plans, and nothing enables them to exercise their child rearing skills, more *than their ability to find and hold a job.* They can then meet the major responsibility that society charges them with—that of taking care of their families."

It is absolutely essential to recognize that a job can never be one's *entire* life—without inviting a possible mental depression. Good health, sexual fulfillment, constructive friends, some meaningful activities, regular entertainment, and relaxing pastimes are vital to maintain mental stability.

Jobs also have important drawbacks and can produce high stress situations.

Women, blacks, Hispanics, Native American Indians, and people of Asiatic origins are struggling for job equality on all levels.

Many women find they are expected to outproduce white males doing equal work, particularly on executive levels.

Dr. Charles Winterhalter, Medical Director of Pitney-Bowes, in Stamford, Connecticut, discovered: "Alcoholism is up among women [and ethnic minorities—THE AUTHORS] in top management. This is definitely job-related." (Alcoholism is destructive "self-medication" for one's mental depression—THE AUTHORS.)

Director of the famed Menninger Foundation, Tobias W. Brocher, reports that although "women tend to have higher psychological and physical endurance for stress" than men—the stresses in being the only woman (or the only ethnic minority member—THE AUTHORS) among the males, causes considerably higher stress.

Director Brocher observes, "Often her reaction is to outdo male counterparts constantly, whether in the number of martinis, the number of tough jokes, or whatever."

Paddy Chayefsky's acclaimed movie, *Network*, stars Faye Dunaway in the role of a rare species—a *top* female TV administrative executive. Her behavior reflects precisely the desperation women executives experience on the job—and its destructive consequences.

Director Brocher explains why this is often the case. "She has no support system on the job. She suffers from isolation. This creates uncertainty over *self-esteem*. And it inevitably ends in *depression*."

Director Brocher points out that the Menninger Foundation's executive mental health seminars (which he supervises) shows a *big increase in women executives* who come for help from job stress:

(YEAR OF 1966)	(YEAR OF 1966)
MALES ATTENDING EXECUTIVE MENTAL HEALTH SEMINARS	WOMEN ATTENDING EXECUTIVE MENTAL HEALTH SEMINARS
100%	**0**

And now in this era when more women are being employed as executives:

(YEAR OF 1976)	*(YEAR OF 1976)*
WOMEN ATTENDING EXECUTIVE MENTAL HEALTH SEMINARS	MALES ATTENDING EXECUTIVE MENTAL HEALTH SEMINARS
80%	**20%**

Jobs can't automatically cure *all* one's key emotional problems. And many jobs are too repetitive and boring.

Too many, who spend the better part of the day at work, can agree with Counselor Roy Walters. Mr. Walters, a job enrichment counselor, reports the rating of the top ten most boring jobs in *The Futurist* magazine:

1. assembly line workers
2. highway toll collectors
3. car-watchers in tunnels
4. typists
5. bank guards
6. copy machine operators
7. setters of bogus type (for paid-for, never-utilized advertisements)
8. computer tape librarians
9. automatic elevator operators
10. childless housewives

Many other boring jobs could be listed that are equally as or even more boring than those listed above.

But—and this is a big "but"—most non-working people will find that it is almost impossible to maintain *daily* varied experiences to equal even the most boring jobs (where there are other people also on the premises). This is why people with mental depression that requires hospitalization generally terminate their depression. The stimuli of psychotherapists, doctors, nurses, occupational therapists, and the other patients end the isolation of the mentally depressed.

It is far better to receive the stimulation of other people on a *job* than in a mental hospital. The job serves as a barrier to mental depression, when employment is available.

Too many millions suffer today from "unemployment shock." After industry rejects the job applicant innumerable times, the unemployed person is unable to tolerate further rejections. He or she becomes job-hunt shy, and gives up the effort to find gainful employment.

"Unemployment shock" can trigger a mental depression. The sufferer needs psychotherapy to overcome the supersensitivity preventing his or her search for employment. Volunteering to work with non-profit-making agencies, without remuneration, may be a useful strategy to maintain social and job skills. Of course, the goal is to use this service as a stepping stone to salaried employment.

Dr. James P. Comer confirms this: "Jobless people are under *great stress*. Society condemns them for not being able to care for themselves and accepting 'handouts.'

"Parents are unable to feel good about themselves. They often take their bad feelings out on each other— parent on parent, parent on child, children on parents.

"Homes of unemployed, frequently unemployed, and marginally employed people are more often chaotic and filled with high conflict than those of people regularly and well employed. Family break-up and movement from place to place in search of a better situation or 'just in front of the rent man' is more likely.

"Communities of yesterday's unemployed and marginally employed are the places where many of today's unemployed will grow up and prepare for adulthood.

"These communities, schools, decaying buildings, and street gangs, are often seething with hopelessness and despair. Here is anger and alienation, apathy, and disruptive behavior.

"What is learned in the unemployed families is not likely to lead to success and good citizenship. It breeds, instead, problems which are paralyzing and destroying our urban areas today."

Good jobs are like oxygen to people. They can't guarantee life will be wonderful—but remove them, and there's no life.

It is important to understand the causes of mental depression in order to speed its termination. One cause of mental depression is the *durability* of trauma (pain) inflicted by a vital loss. The loss can be of a child, a mate, a job, etc.

A study was made of the durability of the trauma that a burning ship had on its surviving crew. About half the crew had survived, many with very severe burns. It was found that even after *five years*, the trauma of this tragic fire negatively affected most of the survivors. It had lessened their ambitions and abilities; they now spent more time ashore than working at sea. The fire at sea lasted for four hours—yet this negatively influenced the majority of the survivors for many years that followed.

The trauma of a serious loss, such as unemployment, takes its toll long after the event appears to be over. And one is more able to deal with this trauma when recognizing the part it plays. Otherwise, one ends up without understanding and is left asking, "Why am I hurting?"

People will work harder to avoid or prevent these serious losses when they know the price it will exact years afterwards.

Depressed patient Tom Allen was caught up in a double bind situation. He was a college student when he started treatment during the late sixties. His prestigious college was in turmoil as its students dissented, protested, and initiated strikes. Many of them wished an end to the Vietnam war.

Mr. Allen was in the forefront of these struggles and was arrested a number of times during these protests. His studies in journalism were interrupted to the degree that he finally dropped out of college.

This was at odds with Mr. Allen's previous scholastic record. He had always been in the top quarter of his class. Very intense, he explained to us: "Any compromise with my principles is a sellout! I don't care how many times I go to jail to get justice in my country!"

In prison, as is often the case, he was gang raped constantly. His rapists were of all ethnic groups, white, black, and Puerto Rican. This confused his sexual image of himself as a masculine figure. He came very close to committing suicide after each sexual attack.

He learned to care *very much* about *not* ending up in prison. Now he's very careful not to get jailed, but his scholastic record of absences has flunked him out of school.

His parents were very worried about his chances as a self-supporting adult, for Tom refused to work for any corporation he considered pro-war. He wanted one that was pro-union, pro-sexual equality, pro-black equality, and a host of other stipulations.

Tom remained unemployed. Adamant, he worked without remuneration for organizations that supported his causes. He told his parents, "I will not sell my soul—working for corporations I can't believe in."

Twice the women he loved parted from him because he had lost sight of the fact that in this world he needs to work to survive. He has to eat, clothe himself, pay rent, pay for entertainment, pay for newspapers, magazines, books—in short, only minors can afford his fiscal life style.

Slowly, Mr. Allen is coming round to recognizing that refusal to compromise regarding one's vocation may also mean no wife, and, ultimately, no respect from anyone.

He's begun to say that he can further his ideals without getting so locked into them that his income vanishes. He observes that it need not be all or nothing at all. He's begun to question the usefulness of the efforts of a friend who is organizing a union that doesn't have a ghost of a chance of succeeding. He's begun to examine possible successes versus hopeless causes.

As Mr. Allen perceives his vulnerability to hopeless extremism, he is developing a readiness to compromise realistically. As he says now: "I think I'm getting ready to compromise—but I've not lost sight of my goals. But I have to learn to not throw myself in a collision course that neither helps me nor my cause."

Now that he is coming to terms with reality, he is setting limits to his illusions of instant change. And his unlimited mental depression is simultaneously showing limits.

When one is unemployed and finds getting a job extremely difficult, that's an *individual* economic depression.

A *social* economic depression is the absence of jobs for vast numbers of people seeking employment.

A *mental* depression is a psychological illness that severely retards one's thinking and emotions. One's skills during a mental depression are slowed down.

Economic and mental depressions are closely linked to each other:

THE DOUBLE HELIX: SIMILAR CHARACTERISTICS OF MENTAL DEPRESSION TO ECONOMIC DEPRESSION (JOBLESSNESS)

MENTAL DEPRESSION

ECONOMIC DEPRESSION

LOSS OF SELF-ESTEEM

LOSS OF SELF-ESTEEM

LOSS OF NORMAL SELF-IDENTITY

LOSS OF NORMAL SELF-IDENTITY

FEELINGS OF HOPELESSNESS

FEELINGS OF HOPELESSNESS TO FIND A JOB

SUICIDAL IDEAS

JOBLESS PERSONS' BELIEF THAT THEY ARE WORTH MORE DEAD, THROUGH INSURANCE MONEY. GOVERNMENTS COMMIT SUICIDE WHEN THEY PERMIT MASSIVE UNEMPLOYMENT TO REACH PROPORTIONS THAT CAUSE REVOLUTION.

LOSS OF SEX DRIVE

LOSS OF SEX DRIVE

LOSS OF APPETITE (OR EXCESSIVE OVEREATING)

LOSS OF APPETITE (OR EXCESSIVE OVEREATING)

The New York Times did an in-depth study of the effects joblessness has on the multimillions of unemployed youth. Their investigation again validated the finding that unemployment triggers a mental depression for many of the jobless.

Testing the universality of the effect of economic depression on the unemployed, *The New York Times** investigated unemployment in Europe, where it is also widespread:

Bitterness and Alienation Grow for
Unemployable, Overtrained

Paris, Dec. 12—Unemployed or unemployable, Agim Likaj in Brussels, Klaus Ledwig in Nuremberg, Kaen Patte in Paris, Gérard Jumel in the Paris Suburb of Nanterre, and many, many others, don't quite know where to turn or how to react in growing bitterness, alienation and *depression . . .*

. . . Gérard Jumel, 22 and newly married, sitting in a crowded cafe near the Nanterre employment office, describes his frustration in trying to find work as an industrial designer. Characterizing himself as nervous and agitated, he says it is a "crime when a society is unable to provide jobs."

*   *   *

Dr. Freud discovered, as did writer Sholom Aleichem, that humor is frequently used as a defense against the severe blows life deals out.

Jewish folk tales originated the story of Reb Mendal, itinerant Polish Rabbi.** He went from impoverished synagogue to impoverished synagogue (where they could not

---

* *The New York Times*, New York, 1976, page 10.
** Writer, anthologist, and raconteur Arthur Tumin heard this story during the great economic depression of the thirties from his father, Rabbi Aryah Y. Tumin, the noted Talmudic authority.

afford to hire a full-time rabbi) to preach on the Sabbath. In return for Reb Mendel's imaginative sermons, the congregation would provide a bed and a meal for the Sabbath.

On the Sabbath, just before Reb Mendel would ascend the *bimah* (stage) to preach, he'd always approach the most affluent member of the congregation. Smiling ingratiatingly, he would politely inquire, "May I borrow 20 rubles from you before I deliver my sermon? I'll return it as soon as I complete my sermon."

The affluent member of the congregation would stare at Reb Mendel as if he had taken leave of his senses. Aghast, he'd sputter indignantly: "But Reb Mendel—it is absolutely forbidden by the Holy Scriptures to carry money on the holy Sabbath! Why, in God's name would you want to commit this monstrous sin?"

Reb Mendel would humbly reply, "You see, Reb Shlomah, after I put the twenty rubles in my pocket—I then can speak with so much more authority than when my pockets are bare!"

*   *   *

The writings of the Jewish Mark Twain, Sholom Aleichem, is the inspiration for the song "If I Were A Rich Man," from *Fiddler on the Roof.* Its lyrics express the essence of Sholom Aleichem's keen understanding of behavior. He observed that life, for the most part and for most people, consisted of the struggle to pay bills.

What Sholom Aleichem had observed 100 years earlier was echoed in *The New York Times* study of European unemployment: ". . . many, many others, don't know quite where to turn or how to react (to joblessness) except in growing bitterness, alienation, and *depression.* . . ."

Mark Twain tells the story of the indigent Eskimo in a tiny Arctic village. The poverty stricken man was ignored by the more affluent when attending the Council of the Elders. When he attempted to speak at the Council a frozen silence greeted his words. No attention was paid to him in his own igloo by his family or his dogs.

When he attempted wit, it was considered clumsy and unfunny. To his children, wife, the suitor of his daughter, the Elders, and the others in the village, this poverty-stricken man was a nonentity.

One bleak day, while he was vainly fishing, he accidentally stumbled on twelve *iron* fish hooks. They had been buried in a snow drift on an ice floe. In the Eskimo economy, an iron fish hook is the equivalent of a giant oil well in Texas.

When the formerly impoverished Eskimo told the village of his find, he was immediately and unanimously elected head of Council of Elders for life. People now came from far and near to hang on his every word. When speaking at the Council, all that he proposed was applauded and unanimously voted for. When he told a joke, everyone howled with laughter and rolled helplessly on the floor, holding their aching sides.

When he was at home, all deferred respectfully to his every wish. This included his dogs.

His daughter's swain had disappeared, having given up all hope of being sufficiently important to win the daughter of this brilliant, superbly acute multimillionaire.

*   *   *

One should differentiate between unemployment due to irresponsible character and *social* unemployment where millions are unemployed, regardless of effort, skills, experience, training, and education. The latter is an economic depression and no shame or guilt should be felt or attributable to the hapless victim. *Social* unemployment is the responsibility of those in charge of the economy in both the public and private sectors. In addition to the multi-blows the unemployed receive, the guilt of the victims, feeling they are the cause of this disastrous unemployment, is *not* appropriate. Yet, the unemployed in an economic depression *do* take on the guilt for the absence of jobs, although they cannot afford falsely to assume the blame. Too many stresses are already at work building toward a potential mental depression.

*   *   *

Dr. Freud discovered that fear of abject poverty is the most universal characteristic of a mental depression throughout the world.

A *society* courts suicide where economic depression is permitted to persist. The economic depression triggers mental depressions, and overburdens too many members of that society, for that nation to survive for long. The vast economic depression that destituted post-World War I Germany, set up so many emotional and social upheavals, that a variety of protesting forces emerged to fight the government and each other. The whole world paid with blood in World War II for the neglected economic depressions that had swept all nations after World War I.

Mental depression generates suicidal thinking in the individual sufferers—economic depression generates national suicide, as protest movements may overthrow the dysfunctioning government that permitted an economic depression to persist.

*   *   *

There is a trend accelerating at a dangerous pace to retire employees in industry who are over fifty years of age.

Until 1945, most American employees remained on the job until they died. Since the end of World War II, this is no longer true. Retirement, involuntary and voluntary, occurs for most older employees.

Social Security and private pension plans have developed a myth in the United States. It is now unrealistically believed that most Americans can afford to retire at 65. This is neither true financially nor *in terms of maintaining mental health.* One need only examine studies of retirees to observe the havoc created in their financial affairs and their physical and mental health.

Experts on the aging process agree with the American Medical Association regarding job retirement. The American Medical Association vigorously *opposes* arbitrary retirement at 65. Their reason for their strong opposition to job retirement at any age is simple. The health of body and mind for most retirees deteriorates rapidly upon retirement.

The American Medical Association and other experts on aging found in their investigations that retirees suffer far more mental depression, and die much earlier, than their peers who remain in their jobs.

Dr. Morris Fishbein, head of the American Medical Association for many years, published a definitive study proving retirees get more mental depressions and die sooner than those who refuse to retire.

Psychotherapist Carl Weiss did studies for Dr. Hyman Weiner for Columbia University's School of Social Work on the effect jobs have on employees with a mental depression. In nearly every instance, the depressed employees (of all ages) were able to terminate their depressions faster by holding onto their jobs.

As a result of these findings, enlightened unions and

business-management especially attempt to help those with a mental depression to retain their jobs. Some of these unions work very closely, and confidentially, with mentally depressed members and their psychotherapists to keep the depressed employees on the job. Trusted coworkers, with the permission of the mentally depressed employee, are told how they may help the depressed employee hold his job while he is fighting to terminate his depression. These trusted coworkers go to lunch with the depressed member, prevent him from becoming isolated from the rest of the employees, and offer the empathic support so desperately needed at this time.

The union also works with the depressed member's family, with the approval of the depressed member and the guidance of the psychotherapist.

Because of these efforts, countless families are being kept from breaking up by divorce and separation. For the family of the mentally depressed employee (who is not under treatment) rarely knew what had been going on in his or her troubled mind.

As a result of this unawareness, they don't understand the desperately lonely, isolated feelings the mental depressive is experiencing. The family gets the false impression that the troubled member is rejecting and ignoring them. This can't be farther from the truth. From the patient's therapists they now learn how to relate to and emotionally support their mentally depressed member. This permits him to more effectively terminate his agonizingly lonely condition.

With the mentally depressed patient's job saved in these ways, not only are his family relationships kept alive, but he is prevented from deteriorating into an isolated recluse.

A young colleague described to us how an older man had made the mistake of accepting the "golden age" retirement myth. Mr. Harrison was a hale and hearty salesman, in his early sixties. His sales route was covered by company car. His territory was the expensive suburbs of Westchester, New York. Over the years, he had built up a profitable clientele among retailers of health foods.

Athletic and lean, bachelor Harrison was the picture of a self-starter. He was a highly respected and active member of a dozen organizations, most of which were concerned with ecology or classical music. He was in correspondence with like-minded people throughout Canada and the United States. He would meet some of these fellow enthusiasts at international conferences on conservation. He would make trips to Albany and Washington, D.C., in delegations to lobby for anti-pollution and wildlife preservation legislation. He recorded concerts as a hobby, and had considerable skill in developing a high quality album library of his favorite compositions. In all the organizations Mr. Harrison played a responsible, organizing role.

Well-educated, with strong cultural and community interests, Mr. Harrison led a richly sociable life. That is, until the day he fractured his leg on a hiking trip.

His foot was put in a cast that extended to mid-thigh. With proper care, his leg was expected to return to full function. After he came home from the hospital with his leg in the cast, he retained a part-time housekeeper. She did the necessary chores a few hours each day while Mr. Harrison was in a wheelchair.

Shortly after the accident, Mr. Harrison made the decision not to return to his job. He considered that his pension and Social Security payments would take care of his financial needs. He also considered that his extensive interests, skills, hobbies, and general curiosity would provide a fulfilling life for him.

However, he was essentially in isolation for the more than three months he spent in his apartment as his fracture healed. This helped trigger a mental depression. His memory, normally very retentive, seemed like a sieve to him. His sleep was brief, and interrupted merely by a bird chirping or a dog barking in the street. He developed chronic fatigue, which was totally alien to his former lifestyle.

His appetite and sex drive disappeared. He became impotent. He felt very weak and had to relearn to walk. His stride ceased to be long and vigorous, becoming rather unsteady and dispirited.

He was too troubled at this point to recognize that there are dozens of books showing exercises he could do in his own bedroom that would have restored the tone to his muscles and the vigor to his walk.

His interest in his varied skills and hobbies also vanished. He now felt mentally too slow to attend the ecology meetings in which he had previously played a leadership role. Previously he generated prolific ideas at the meetings and delegations; now he felt he had no ideas to verbalize or contribute.

He felt too embarrassed to attend the organizations dedicated to promoting classical music. Here too, he felt mentally slow and blocked.

Each day he resolved he'd attend his organizations' meetings—when he felt a little "smarter." But spending each day in isolation, he felt more retarded.

He had reached the point where he began to believe that, because of the slowness of his mental faculties, it might be too humiliating ever to return to his former friends in the world of ecology and music.

The correspondence from his acquaintances from all over the country piled up. He felt too empty and apathetic to try to answer the letters. Each day he would look at the increasing pile of unanswered letters and feel emotionally more depleted.

In desperation, he arranged to see our young psychotherapist colleague. At the first session, in short, halting sentences delivered in a monotone, Mr. Harrison related his feelings, his problems, and his history leading up to his mental depression.

Before leaving the psychotherapist's office, Mr. Harrison, sighing frequently, said he might call for another session. The psychotherapist asked him why he "might" call, since it was obvious he needed help urgently. He could not convince Mr. Harrison to make a definite appointment for the following day.

The psychotherapist said, "Mr. Harrison, you are very aware you need psychotherapy. What's stopping you from arranging here and now to get it?"

Mr. Harrison's face was wooden, impassive, emotionless: the classic mask of depression. He turned his lacklustre eyes to the therapist and replied, "Because I feel so helpless and hopeless, I just find making any decision more than I can manage to do. This includes even arranging at this moment to see you tomorrow for treatment. You see, I can't really be sure what I'll do tomorrow until tomorrow comes. Right now, everything I may do is pretty uncertain to me.

"So I can't tell what I'll do or how I'll feel until tomorrow."

The psychotherapist asked Mr. Harrison, "Are you thinking of committing suicide?"

For the first time, Mr. Harrison acted with some outward emotion. In a determined tone he answered, "No. I do not plan to kill myself."

But he persisted in not making a decision to continue therapy.

Finally the psychotherapist concluded the session. "Mr. Harrison, either way, will you call me to let me know whether you plan to continue therapy with me? I'll be here until three tomorrow."

Mr. Harrison remained indecisive. Tomorrow would have to come before he would know what to do.

He departed, leaving a very concerned psychotherapist.

When Mr. Harrison did not call by three the next day, the psychotherapist phoned his apartment. There was no answer. The psychotherapist immediately and rapidly drove the eleven miles to Mr. Harrison's apartment.

There was a police car, empty, in front of Mr. Harrison's high-rise apartment building.

The psychotherapist knocked on the door of Mr. Harrison's twenty-fifth floor apartment. A tear-stained relative of Mr. Harrison admitted him. Behind the weeping woman stood several grim-faced male members of the family. Seated at the table, a sympathetic, young police officer was filling out a report.

Mr. Harrison had overdosed with two bottles of sleeping pills at eleven that morning. The housekeeper found him dead in bed when she let herself in at one.

The psychotherapist informed the stunned relatives what he knew, for the record. As he was departing, he was intercepted at the door by the deceased man's brother.

The brother said pleadingly, "It was very kind of you to have come, but would you do my family another favor? Please, other than to the government, don't let anyone know my brother died from suicide. We'll tell people it was a stroke."

Mr. Harrison had been a bright and responsible man until his mental depression started. Unfortunately Mr. Harrison did *not* understand the vital importance his job played in *maintaining his mental stability.*

Mr. Harrison certainly recognized that his job provided the money to pay his bills—but it is clear he never understood that a job acts as a *structure* for most people's mental stability.

In addition to jobs providing the money for daily necessities, jobs perform the following *survival services.*

Nearly all jobs ensure that people *won't become isolated recluses.* Jobs automatically allow the development of relationships with other people that usually go deeper than saying hello to a neighbor and commenting on the weather.

Jobs ensure some structure to one's life pattern. It requires one to sleep over a certain period; and get up to get to work at another organized period. It avoids the chaos some non-working people develop by sleeping at odd hours, awaking at irregular times, and generally becoming disorganized in other functions as well.

Jobs structure one's dining pattern. Before going to work, some snack or breakfast is regularly eaten. A fairly regular lunch hour is developed on the job. Finally, after work, it's functional to eat dinner. Those not in jobs may tend, if they are not organized, to skip meals, eat at any hour, and generally develop a lifestyle unstructured enough to interfere with their digestive pattern.

Jobs require one to attend to one's grooming in an efficient manner. On the job, grooming and clothes require more care to help to ensure the approval of those one works with.

A job makes one feel needed. Many jobs depend on other people doing part of the work to allow one to complete one's own section of the product or service.

Activities on the job are not only more stimulating than watching TV or waxing the floors, but one has the events that occurred on the job as a topic of conversation. Whether it's at a cocktail party, or over dinner, some conversations will depend on subjects that occurred at work.

People use their jobs to build an important part of their identity. Two big questions that help establish a person's identity for other people are "What does he (or she) do for a living?" and "For whom do they work?"

And let's not lose sight of the iron law that makes jobs so vital—a working person has a feeling of independence, and a non-working person is called *a dependent.*

Even people with secure private, independent incomes (who nevertheless are employed), feel a paying job demonstrates that *they are indeed worth something* to their employers. (This is also true for people without private, independent incomes.) The wealthy working person also benefits from all the other reasons that often make a job a sanity preserver.

It is equally important not to perceive jobs as *perfect places* to cure all of one's ills. Far from it! Nearly all jobs generate tension and stress. Some jobs have built-in occupational diseases that are certain to shorten one's life (miners' work, for example).

Therefore, it is both *realistic* and *distressing* to consider jobs as the foundation for most people's mental stability. But that, at least for the present, is the human condition. Facing this reality means training for the best job you can get. There are other necessities you must deal with in order to prevent a mental depression. Holding a job is just one of them—but for most people, there's no mental survival without one.

Actually, most people must have a job *as long as they live*. This is their first line of defense against mental depression. Their survival, in most instances, depends on their avoidance of early retirement.

It has been found that the majority of older people are both mentally and physically in condition to work. Most of our legislators, judges, and heads of companies are in their sixties and older. Physically and mentally, they are well able to do their work effectively.

Simply because an employee reaches beyond middle age is no ground for compulsory retirement. Business Consultant J. Roger O'Meara, author of *Retirement: Reward or Rejection?*, finds, "People just don't age the same way. Some are old at 18. And others are young at 80."*

To the question, "Should employees be made to retire after a certain age?," Mr. O'Meara discovered the answer is "No."

He discloses why: "Forced retirement causes needless waste of manpower and money. It thrusts an oppressive burden on society."

The investigations made by Mr. O'Meara on the effects of retirement find it is, for the vast majority, a "hellish existence."

His studies on retirement disclose "it usually involves a sharp drop in income. It may also bring loneliness, *depression*, failing health, excessive drinking, and even suicide."

Confirmation of business consultant J. Roger O'Meara and the authors' research are studies by the American Medical Association: The AMA diagnoses compulsory retire-

---

* J. Roger O'Meara, *Retirement: Reward or Rejection?* Report by The Conference Board, a business research organization, 1977.

ment to be, often, as fatal as untreated rabies. It reports: "The sudden cessation of productive work and earning power (by retiring), often leads to physical and emotional deterioration. This in turn leads to premature death.

The American Medical Association means business when it compares retirement with a near-fatal disease. They are fighting compulsory retirement for employees beyond middle age. They charge that retirement significantly helps to induce mental depression and a host of other maladies; this is charged in a legal brief designed to end compulsory retirement.

In spite of this undisputed evidence of the pathology of retirement, the dismissing of older employees proceeds at an ever-increasing pace:

YEAR	% OF EMPLOYEES 45 YEARS OR OLDER
1950	80%
1960	66%

YEAR	% OF EMPLOYEES 65 YEARS OR OLDER
1950	40%
1975	20%

Presently, U.S. laws, by implication, treat older employees as expendable—by *omitting* protection of them in legislation prohibiting discrimination in employment. The Federal law, the Age Discrimination Act of 1967, protects only ages from 40 through 64. There is no protection against age discrimination for the 21,000,000 Americans over 65 years of age. At this writing, Congress may pass a bill prohibiting forcible retirement of employees under 70 years of age.

This still permits millions to remain unprotected from

forced retirement. The resulting millions of mental depressions from these mandatory retirements cannot be excused. It will continue to cost our nation dearly in trying to rehabilitate the lives of these millions over 70 years of age.

The American Jewish Congress offers programs to help those who want jobs and are over 40, and it fights discrimination against all minorities seeking jobs. Satirically, AJC describes those over 40 who are job-seeking as "white niggers."

The courts of this country have, for the most part, joined in discriminating against older employees. Recently, by 7 to 1, the U.S. Supreme Court of Massachusetts ruled that Massachusetts can retire state police who are over 50.

Depriving the older employees not only denies them their inalienable right to pursue jobs on an equal basis, it also falsely perpetuates the myth that older employees are less productive than younger ones. The fact is that older employees are *equally productive*, according to studies made by government, private industry, and universities. (This excludes jobs where heavy physical labor is required. Since most jobs today are non-manual, and with our very sophisticated technology, the days of backbreaking labor are the exception rather than the rule in industry.)

The investigations record that learning ability does *not* decrease significantly with age. On the contrary, older employees generally use better judgment than those who are younger. Steady, organized work patterns are characteristic of older employees. Industry does itself a huge disservice by barring the older employees from retaining their jobs.

The older people have begun to recognize the fraudulent myth that characterizes them as incompetent employees. The American Association of Retired People has joined the American Medical Association in the struggle for equal job rights for older people. Many older people are aware of the danger of the possible mental depression that joblessness frequently induces. Equally, they do not accept the myth of senility as the fate of older people. They are beginning to see that active, employed older people can easily perform their jobs as well as younger employees. They also note that the so-called "senility" is actually mental depression that frequently affects the jobless *young and old*.

As younger employees refuse to accept being junked as obsolescent and unfit to work, so are alert older employees resisting compulsory retirement.

PART TWO

WHY MENTAL DEPRESSION NEED NOT KILL ITS VICTIMS

20 ACTS
THAT HELP END MENTAL DEPRESSION:

1/ Strive for *some personal power.*
2/ Strive for *personal independence; and when necessary, get help from others.*
3/ Strive for *your own welfare constantly.*
4/ Strive for *the welfare of others.*
5/ Strive for *reasonable economic solvency.*
6/ Strive for *continuous resistance to anyone acting to injure you.*
7/ Strive for *others to respect you.*
8/ Strive for *a positive value system.*
9/ Strive for *a network of close relatives and friends.*
10/ Strive for *a fulfilling sex life.*
11/ Strive for *a job that is rewarding.*
12/ Strive for *doing things well while recognizing that you will win some and lose some.*
13/ Strive for *the ability to forgive yourself for occasional errors, moments of cowardice and lapses in being fair to others.*
14/ Strive for *recognizing the fact that the mind has a powerful, self-healing mechanism. All it needs is time and your effort to relate to people.*
15/ Strive for *the avoidance of false guilts.*
16/ Strive for *realistic expectations instead of impossible fantasies that result in massive disappointments.*
17/ Strive for *tackling only one big problem at a time, instead of getting overwhelmed by many that may accumulate.*
18/ Strive for *feeling you're accomplishing something at each step of the whole task.*
19/ Strive for *a healthy body to contain a healthy mind. Healthy diet, exercise, and sleep are all musts.*
20/ Strive for *daily practice of the above acts, in order to effectively defend yourself against mental depression.*

CHAPTER

VIII

WHAT TO DO *NOW*, IF YOU HAVE A CLINICAL MENTAL DEPRESSION

FORCE YOURSELF TO EAT REGULAR, BALANCED MEALS, RE-gardless of your appetite or attitude. This is a physical act which must be done to avoid physical weakness and physical illness.

Physical weakness makes one feel mentally depressed. It also makes one feel older and less able to think and act competently.

Physical illness is to be avoided, both in itself, and because it often helps trigger mental depression. When one already has a mental depression, physical illness exaggerates mental depression because *depression equals loss of power.*

There are a few physical health rules to help ward off physical illness:

Eat balanced, non-fattening meals.
Get sufficient rest and sleep.
Dress functionally in cold climates.
Apply commonsense safety precautions outdoors (e.g. in traffic) and in the home.

Exercise regularly; see your doctor for exercises if you've a disability; daily exercise adds power to your body's strength; and it makes your body *feel* more adequate. Get a physical check-up twice a year.

Absolutely *make* yourself go to bed at a reasonable hour. Read in bed, if need be, to occupy yourself while waiting for the elusive sleep to arrive. Stay in bed for the six, seven, or eight hours your body and mind require. *But don't overstay in bed.* You'll not be rested by overstaying in bed—this is an illusion that tempts the fatigued mental depressive.

You must not put off going to bed at a reasonable hour. We know that your day is frustrating, with so little joy and so much agony, but staying up very late at night to see if you can eke out some fun at the last minute is self-defeating. Either get your fun during your waking hours, or seek it once more after a good night's rest.

Visit a good psychotherapist who will help you develop strategies that will reduce and finally terminate your depression. The therapist may also put you on an antidepressant pill program. Take the pills only as prescribed—don't miss taking them when you're told to take them. *And don't take more than you're ordered to!* It's dangerous and it does not speed recovery or the feeling of well-being—it slows both down.

Antidepressant pills hasten the depression's end. Although they won't get rid of the whole depression, they are a powerful help in ending it. These pills also act to relax you so that you can enjoy restful sleep. During a depression, use every help you can get to end it.

Not infrequently, the therapist's most important role can be to discover in the patient's family an extended network of genuinely resourceful people. These may have a commitment and a sense of some responsibility towards the depressed person. The therapist can, by advice, as well as by acting as a role model, help concerned people to expand their repertoire of knowledge and to determine how to be most helpful.

Very often the therapist can prevent concerned people from developing empty, useless gestures of help towards the depressed victim. These misguided efforts could deteriorate into pain, anger, despair and a sense of resignation in the network of significant others. The therapist can structure well-intentioned efforts into something realistically constructive for the depressive.

The therapist must meet with significant members of the family, in order to enlist them in helping to overcome the patient's mental depression. This is done with the permission of the patient. Nobody is brought into the confidence of the psychotherapist, or presented with patient's problems, except in order to be of help in terminating the depression.

Infrequently, therapists may discover within a family and extended network of significant others a core of malignant enmity and destructiveness. This may be someone closely connected to the depressed person.

But usually, the more we explore behavior conducive to developing depression, the more it's evident that the depressed person is experiencing relationships to which he may have unconsciously largely contributed. For example, one may consciously hide one's real feelings from another, yet simultaneously feel the need to be understood by that person! One is going to be disapppointed at not being understood—yet miserable at self-exposure.

Members of the family may be of great help—or disservice—if they are not advised professionally. James Stone, a 22-year-old college graduate was hospitalized for mental depression when he could no longer function outside. After he recovered, he was due to be discharged. His parents wanted to give a party in honor of his homecoming. Their guest list included many relatives, friends, and school associates.

James, who had hit rock bottom emotionally only a few months previously, was indecisive whether the party should be held. It was decided that he would be under too much pressure to respond to this sort of affair. The patient, the therapist, and the family had discussed it and came to this decision.

If family therapy had not been practiced, this party might have been given and resulted in too much unnecessary stress on James. In the popular movie, *A Woman Under the Influence,* the wife returning from the mental hospital, is given a surprise party by her jubilant husband. The pressure on her to respond to all the well-wishers is too great. She has a serious relapse. Here, instead of the family's being a valuable resource for the recovery of the mental patient, it became the cause of increased stress.

One of our mentally depressed patients told her husband she was ready to see a Broadway play. He selected tickets to a hit musical. The wife then suggested they eat at a very popular dining place. After standing in the restaurant, waiting for nearly an hour, in a crowd resembling that in a rush-hour subway, it was too much for the wife. They had to go home; they skipped dinner and theatre. They had attempted too much. *Yet they learned* for the next time to park in a quieter street and take a taxi to a small, unhurried restaurant. From there, a relaxed ride to the theatre—and the wife would not have to meet the challenge of jostling crowds, close quarters, and hurried entrances and exits. That type of stress could come later, when she was eventually ready for it.

Significant others can make an important difference in the recovery rate of the mentally depressed. Those people important to the patient must be included in the patient's activities. Recovery from mental depression can utilize *some* challenging situations—but these have to be judiciously planned, not overdone.

Significant others can be of great help in speeding the end of the patient's depression if they recognize that the patient has not *lost* his or her essential abilities and mental strengths. They are still present, though the person may be more lethargic than formerly. Therefore, they should not talk *down* to the patient. People are very aware when they are addressed in a tone of voice which implies they have regressed to second childhood.

People close to the mentally depressed try to offer directions to them when they neglect proper diet, sleep, intake of medication, etc. It requires great care on the part of these significant people to assure the patient that the anti-depressant medication and healthy physical living will require time before they take an effect in helping to terminate the depressed condition. Unfortunately, these measures don't act immediately to help lift the mental depression and the patient must be apprised of this fact.

Anti-depressant medication helps the patient to sleep better, and in time helps the depression to lift.

The importance of involving relatives and friends in aiding the mentally depressed to get out of that condition is uppermost in our treatment strategy. When we see a patient in a clinical depression, we check whether there are parents, mates, or siblings whom we may enlist to help the patient.

We always work out out beforehand with the depressed patient whether these relatives can be called upon. The patient recognizes that he or she cannot live out his or her life successfully by getting constant emotional and financial help from his relatives. But if this is an emergency situation, or a new situation, there may be people who are prepared, temporarily, to act in a supportive role.

Our job is to point out to the depressed patient that it is legitimate to use people in an emergency—but not to use them up. One does not ask the relatives for a loan of two thousand dollars for the depressed patient—at least not without a note or even possibly interest. But you can call on the relative to get together for an evening . . . for a walk or a movie—it takes the patient "out of himself," providing temporary relief from his misery.

One of the things we always tell our depressed patients is, "In your current depressed condition, you're not good company for yourself. You'll catch yourself reliving all the 'dumb' things you did during the day.

"Mix your thoughts with others. If it's too much of a strain, be a listener or a low-key participant with others.

"With someone present to relate to, you won't have a total opportunity to keep thinking obsessively of what you're doing wrong that's causing your depression. Alone, you can find limitless junk to dredge up while in your present state of mind.

"Your social mixing with one or more people is absolutely vital during your depression and your increased sociability will speed up the termination of the depression. Good ideas, stimulated by company, may surface in you and be reinforced to produce more.

"Establish connections with other people. You prolong your depression as long as you remain cloistered."

A very frequent problem depression generates for its victim is that his capacity to perform, respond, and assume responsibility may change almost minute by minute, and this happens without apparent cause. Consequently, he may be caught up in an endless debate with himself, "Can I, or don't I want to?"

Those around him may also become confused by these variations in the depressed person's personality. How this dilemma is dealt with is most important. In it's crudest terms, it seeks to know, "Am I faking, or not?" If this dilemma persists to a significant degree, professional therapy of a more intensive kind may be required.

Don't *consciously* hate yourself for your present poorer functioning. *You* are your present self. *Don't reject yourself.* Don't play the huge mansion-owner who fires an incompetent servant. Don't fire yourself through suicide, because you are not satisfied with your performance. Remember, the servant can be replaced; when a person commits suicide, then nothing is left to be replaced!

Love yourself. See yourself as *temporarily* handicapped. It's as if you were down with a high fever.

Or perhaps instead of "love yourself," accept the fact that you're in a depressed condition, *without blaming yourself or others.*

Don't spend time looking around for others to blame for your depression; it's self-defeating. You waste a lot of useful energy ruminating how your mother, father, lover, mate, boss, co-worker did you in. Rather than focusing your anger and hatred on any of them (even if they helped develop your depression), work out strategies not to allow them to interfere with your functioning effectively.

Your survival means protecting other people. It is similar to a military situation where survival is most precarious. For your own protection, you may have to protect the well-being of the scout ahead of you.

Your survival depends on helping others survive—"no man is an island unto himself."

In certain cases mental depression permeates the household and immobilizes all. One's wife may become a poor lover as a result, or a poor mother to one's children— and that's not a survival technique.

You don't expect, nor do others expect you, to function like a vigorous person, when you're down with the 'flu. So, equally, pamper yourself when you're down with a mental depression. You'd do it if you were down with pneumonia.

Don't sneer at yourself for your *temporary*, massive mental depression. Don't put yourself down because you're temporarily less productive. Don't accuse yourself for your lower spirits. We have sufficient putdown artists in this world; don't adopt this negative attitude towards yourself.

Keep working at making points wherever you find yourself. Keep plugging, even though the points you rack up may be less than what you customarily achieve when you enjoy better mental health.

On your job, in your household chores, with friends old or new, at parties—wherever you happen to be—keep pushing. This *fight* tactic generates greater and greater feelings of adequacy. It strengthens your abilities to cope.

Keep your expectations of life on a realistic, modest level. Particularly during a clinical mental depression, one tends to have too-high expectations of oneself and of life. Instead, be pleasantly surprised with each victory that happens during the day.

Take on one task at a time. Finish it and try the next one. Don't make excessive demands on the quality and the quantity of your work. It's enough that you run your daily race over the hurdles that are always there.

Drop the excessive burden of saving others when your depression is endangering your own survival. This does not mean you should turn into a barracuda in order to terminate your clinical mental depression. *That* will result in an additional burden of having to constantly protect your back.

But now, of all times, you must keep your head above water. After you return to your former, better-functioning self, you can realistically then see who else you can help keep afloat.

Keep your body trim. Maintain a well-groomed appearance. There is likely to be less stress when you present a finer exterior to the world.

Watch your value system so that you don't experience extra guilt during this trying time of massive depression. Play it safe. When in doubt about the morality or dignity of a situation—protect yourself! Don't deliberately put yourself into a vulnerable position which might foster guilty feelings.

Part of the unnerving guilt of many in a clinical mental depression is the perplexing question, "Why me—why should I be punished with this depression?"

The person in the depths of the clinical mental depression often feels tormented *with no clear sense*: "Why am *I* being picked on to get this mental depression?"

The perplexed victims of the depression take stock of what they have—and they may see themselves as having a fine mate or lover, nice children, a good job, a desirable home, and so on. "What," they ask, "is wrong with me— why don't I appreciate these real blessings I possess?" This perplexity makes them feel that their depression is illegitimate.

These confused people are frequently in the position of the youngster who has neither a good set of parents nor a bad pair. These parents give out confusing messages and cues to their child. They blow hot and cold by turns—and the child can't get set to tolerate their sudden switches. The parents are indulgent, then they become very strict. They permit today what they forbid tomorrow. They love now, later they become very hostile to the perplexed youngster. The fragile child can't dig his heels in and deal with these unstable home conditions.

The parents have put the child in that paralyzing state called a double bind. The child would actually have been better off if the parents were openly and consistently hostile. The child would then have known where he or she stands, and would then have been able to build defenses for this clear-cut state. The youngster would have tightened his or her belt and known where the attack would be coming from. You can't avoid blows you can't see coming at you.

The same goes for many people suffering with a clinical mental depression. They're not at all sure from where they are being hit—so they neither have their defenses up nor can counterattack. The role of the competent psychotherapist is to help you clear up where the blows are coming from—what caused your depression; and these causes can be ignored only if one is willing to pay the painful price of mental depression. It is never too soon for the mentally depressed to dispel their perplexity regarding the causes of mental depression.

"Loosening up" is not a license to do something extreme you can ill afford, depressed or otherwise! Some people suffering from clinical mental depression go on a spending spree to try to terminate their depression. They put aside their judgment and do something self-defeating.

Others in the throes of a mental depression attempt exploiting others. They take advantage of their victims in an inhumane way. They are setting into motion actions that will ultimately isolate them from others. They are intensifying their depression—or setting up the basis for another depression.

To loosen up usefully, in or out of a mental depression, it is advisable to give up obsessive, perfectionist strivings. These are neither productive nor calculated to maintain the support of family or friends.

Stay loose and flexible by not judging yourself harshly at this time. Apply "Judge not, lest you be judged!" to your own self. This doesn't mean you avoid serious, mature responsibilities. It does mean you won't *seek out* collision-course confrontations in your present state. You are already working on the shock produced by a clincal depression. So you are presently taking on no *additional battles* that do not urgently need to be fought. Like any experienced boxer, you don't want to fight more than you can handle.

As you rebuild your emotional power, you'll increase the number of battles to win more goals. All the battles will still be there awaiting you. Once your body and mind feel more like your former, able self—you'll do some mopping up on the battlefield.

A fairly usual depressive's recovery pattern of returning to one's former power is told to us by Arlene Judson:

"My mental depression overwhelmed me and transformed me into a terrified, irrational person. It was so intense, I had to be hospitalized in a psychiatric hospital. I was treated there for nearly a year.

"During this time, relatives, friends, and fellow employees from the corporation visited me. They came to show their interest and support for me, and their hopes that I'd recover.

"After I was discharged from the hospital I was treated by a psychotherapist and continued on antidepressant pills.

"I returned to my former job as office manager. I had been with this firm for fifteen years. Very fortunately, the corporation had been fair and held my job open for me. They recognized I hadn't been malingering.

"There are two cousins in my firm (no relationship to me). One is secretary to the chairman of the board, the other to the president of the company.

"These two decided that I was too timid to maintain my former status on the job. They promptly proceeded to order me about, in front of the other employees, as well as in private. Their job description did not give them this authority, but I felt too inadequate to stand up to them or bring this issue up to my executive superior.

"Each night as I went to bed I wondered, 'Will tomorrow morning be the day I'll awaken to my former competent self? If it is so—I'll put a quick stop to those two cousins who've become my self-appointed bosses!'

"A few months after I'd gone back to work, one morning I awakened—and I felt I *was* my former, adequate self!

"I welcomed my 'real me' back, and literally sauntered into the office.

"There were the two inseparable cousins with a written and verbal list of chores for me—that their job required *them* to do.

"I was handed the list; which I tossed lightly into a wastebasket before their eyes. I murmured amiably, 'Please don't bother me with your duties, I have my job to do.'

"The cousins eyed each other. They looked carefully at me, as if for the first time they saw me. Whatever they saw convinced them. Without a word they retreated.

"They invite me to lunch with them now and then. I do likewise. They haven't bothered me since; and that took place over a year ago."

As in the cases of most people who suffer from a clinical mental depression, Arlene's symptoms cleared up. She had returned to her previous pattern of taking care of herself.

In a report we did for Dr. Hyman Weiner of Columbia University, we documented how his program of keeping mentally depressed employees *on their job* generally hastened the ultimate termination of their clinical mental depression.

Arlene's return to work substantially aided in her recovery of her former coping skills. In most cases, holding on to the job did more to overcome the mental depression condition than a "vacation" from the job. Not the least of the benefits from hanging in on the job are the essential payments for food, clothing, shelter, and psychotherapeutic treatment for the depression.

Arlene had gained realistic insight with regard to clinical mental depression's causes, effects, and cure. She said, "I no longer take for granted my present state of coping adequately with stresses and problems of daily living. I believe I won't naively repeat the actions that brought on my mental depression.

"However, I've gotten more sophisticated about mental depression. Just as I'm never fully discharged by my family doctor or my dentist, I visit my psychotherapist twice a year for a mental health check-up. This way I can find whether I'm dealing realistically with life, or getting precariously close to the edge of the cliff of wishful fantasizing."

Very often, after leaving the immobilization of a clinical mental depression, the recovered patients undertake too many activities to compensate for the past. They overcompensate and overload their capacities. Like a student who neglected to study until a few days before the big exam, former depressives try to catch up on lost activities.

Just as the late crammer may fail to overtake his studies, the former depressives are likely not to succeed in the projects that require five times their potential. This is likely to act as a depressant. It may become an important factor in generating a subsequent depression.

Some students, after doing poorly because of their undisciplined study habits, vow to get straight A's for the following three years. This is as pressure-generating as waiting for the last minute to study. Both overload the tension tolerance of the mind and body.

When you work out from the clinical depression—you *can* be stronger than before you developed it. For if you are conscious of how clinical depression is developed, you can avoid the next bout with it. Whatever the goals, money (products and services) must be present. Forgetting this one truth alone, for a significant time, is sufficient cause for developing a clinical mental depression.

Protect yourself from clinical depression by acquiring a job role that gives you some dignity and self-respect. Without this, some people are steered into a depression. And when you have this constructive job, work energetically to hold onto it. It merits a great deal of tender loving care to maintain your job security. *Many people* are *their job.* The loss of a significant job, and inability to get another like it, may mean the eventual loss of emotional stability.

Medical and dental preventive care are signals, to both your conscious and unconscious mind, that you are protecting yourself.

Act to protect your value system on which your dignity depends for its survival. Your emotions start to get significantly depressed when your value system and its protection are not both functioning for your survival.

Don't hesitate to stop procedures that demean or dehumanize you. Regardless how long this destructive situation has been going on—stop it! It's never too late to call a halt to the downhill trip of your emotions caused by attacks on your self-respect.

CHAPTER

IX

HOW TO AVOID
THE NEXT
CLINICAL DEPRESSION

DON'T TAMPER WITH YOUR SLEEP REQUIREMENTS. GET A full night's sleep every night. Everything will be there in the morning that you didn't get to the day before.

Eat balanced meals and avoid becoming overweight. As a result you'll be healthier and more energetic, while looking better.

Maintain good grooming. It boosts your spirits and those of whomever you are in contact with.

Always protect your own true interests as your first priority. A clinical depression is *telling* you loud and clear that you are neglecting your own real interests.

Money must always be around to protect you. Accept no substitute for it. Neither ideologies nor fantasies making counter proposals in the place of money can ever save you where money is absent.

During a mental depression you can carefully attempt to regain your dignity. Just as Rome took a while to build —it will take time to rebuild your life where it is presently being abused. No matter how slowly, as long as you're consistently rebuilding your dignity, your spirits will rise with it.

A most vital area in avoiding mental depression is *knowing how to handle compromises.* A compromise requires surrendering something of value that the compromiser prizes. The amount of the surrender and its importance to the compromiser is most critical.

Some compromises may be useful, necessary for survival, and genuinely constructive. Our patient, Ann Sohmer, is nearly recovered from a clinical mental depression. She works as a designer of books in a publishing company.

Recently, a new senior designer was hired by Ms. Sohmer's firm. He was assigned the job that Ms. Sohmer had been led to believe by her superior would be hers.

Ms. Sohmer felt betrayed, bypassed. She measured the new designer's abilities and felt that she was more competent. Ms. Sohmer considered resigning her job.

However, she recognized that jobs were then exceedingly scarce. Ms. Sohmer depended on her salary to maintain her apartment and other necessities of life.

She did not obey her strong impulse to resign angrily.

This compromise—remaining on the job despite her frustrated expectations—shows she is dealing constructively with reality. Ms. Sohmer feels very angry at her superior who has hired the new senior designer over her. It takes strong willpower for Ms. Sohmer to smile cordially at her superior; yet she does.

Ms. Sohmer is experienced enough to know that sullen employees generally don't last long on the job. So she does not play games that may weaken her hold on her job.

A recognition that she had not acted in a demeaning way here is firm in Ms. Sohmer's mind. She believes, instead, that she had rolled with the punch. Her pride had not blinded her to the necessity of holding her job.

Meanwhile, Ms. Sohmer is energetically and discreetly

hunting for a new comparable job. She realistically recognizes that remaining on her present job is a dead end. But until she finds one equal to it, she is not unrealistically burning her financial bridges behind her.

Fortunately for Ms. Sohmer, other aspects of the job are not substantially abrasive. She can live with the present job, while looking for another one offering more opportunities.

Unfortunately, there are other kinds of compromise. *Some compromises are very destructive, and may contribute substantially to a clinical mental depression.*

Jim Dirken, just over his mental depression, had a new management take over where he was employed. Mr. Dirken is an experienced technical scientific writer. Within a few days after meeting the new head of the firm, Mr. Dirken had an unpleasant confrontation with him. In front of other employees, the new head mocked Mr. Dirken's stutter. He informed Mr. Dirken that he does not "have time to waste when verbally communicating."

Mr. Dirken carefully observed that this insulting behavior by the new president was not a whim. It was rather the new boss's operational strategy.

Mr. Dirken promptly looked for a new job. Fortunately a new one in another firm opened up for him in a few days. Had it not, Mr. Dirken had planned to confront the new head at the next instance of unequivocal personal abuse. Either the boss would have changed his personnel policy—or Mr. Dirken would have defined the situation openly. He would have charged the executive with covert firing in the guise of administering the business. Had Mr. Dirken quietly submitted to this outrageous treatment by his boss, his emotional stability would have paid too high a price for the compromise.

Important compromises—those that deal with one's essential dignity, integrity, basic values—must not be stretched too far. For then the compromise storms one's own inner citadel. One must differentiate between *constructive and destructive compromises*. For this area is one of the pillars supporting one's survival.

In civilized society, many compromises are essential. As people live in society, of necessity they will meet with the need for some repressions, inhibitions, and frustrations. They will find some delays necessary, rather than seeking instant gratification.

However, the important thing is to learn which compromises are necessary and constructive and which are unnecessary because they are destructive. Those who underestimate the importance of carefully thinking things through before compromising are unaware of the power compromises exert on mental stability and mental depression.

Guilt feelings play many roles with regard to mental depressions. People often regret an action against another because it induces guilt. They attempt to erase this guilt by apologizing to the offended party and they hope the matter ends there.

It does not always work quite so simply.

Edmond Grant is a patient with a clinical mental depression. He frequently accuses his teenage son of misdeeds. When Mr. Grant finds that his wallet has apparently been rifled, he quickly accuses his son. Later, when Mr. Grant discovers he had paid a bill with the missing money, he has to apologize to his son.

Each time this occurs, Mr. Grant has some guilt to erase.

These *frequent* apologies do not remove all the guilt. Every time that Mr. Grant makes a groundless accusation against his wife, his son, and his fellow employees, he has to offer an apology, hat in hand.

Mr. Grant doesn't find a release from his anxieties, fears, and frustrations by his unreasonable charges against significant people in his life. Instead, he finds he's multiplied his stresses.

By "taking it out on others" (hostility displacement), new guilts are bred. It helps thrust the doer into greater emotional and behavioral immobilization.

Charles Dawson, forty-eight, came to us with some awareness of the causes of his mental depression. He informed us that his wife recently lost the use of her legs in an auto accident.

Mr. Dawson's firm has gone bankrupt; he's been looking for a job for the past five months. His wife's injuries have put them into very heavy debt. They have five children; only the eldest is working.

Mr. Dawson had been going to evening college and was very near to his masters degree in sociology. Not only can he no longer afford to complete it, there are very few jobs today that his degree can obtain. This has frustrated his long-hoped-for goal of teaching in a college.

These severe stresses brought on others. It reached the low point where Mr. Dawson felt he was unable to cope with his daily problems. Since the outside, environmental stresses are so clearcut, Mr. Dawson is suffering a *reactive* depression. He *reacted* to specific, overt stresses that substantially caused his mental depression.

Mr. Dawson's therapy is removing his unreal expectations about what life should offer him. Life is no promised land of rose gardens. Accidents can happen to one's mate. Careers can get blocked. Frustrations over these stresses need not cause psychopathological reactions. As Mr. Dawson develops more realistic expectations of what life may bring, he is in a strong position to avoid future mental depressions.

Unlike Mr. Dawson, whose case involved *obvious* stresses, Ms. Barbara Turner, twenty-two, told us she could see no apparent causes for her mental depression.

She taught adolescents in a prison and she believed she was providing a very useful service. She was halfway through her master's degree in education and went to classes in the evenings.

Ms. Turner was engaged to a law student and said she loved him. Despite her mental depression, she felt her health was satisfactory. She considered herself attractive, and she was—although her unsmiling face and drawn expression reflected the stress she was experiencing.

Our task was to help Ms. Turner unearth the causes of her mental depression. Then we would be able to work on eliminating them. (Where the causes that are responsible for a mental depression are obscure, it is called an *endogenous* depression.)

At first, Ms. Turner was proud of the work she was doing as a teacher of adolescent boys in prison. Later on, she revealed *that her class was out of control.* This she had been denying to herself, deluding herself that her teaching methods were "progressive" or "alternate education."

In therapy, she no longer repressed this conflict from her consciousness. She then took measures regarding this serious problem. She also examined whether she was neglecting her studies for her master's degree by funnelling all her energies into her job. She found that she had been failing in her university classes and that her hopes of eventually becoming a school principal were becoming unreal.

Ms. Turner discovered that she had been failing in her

graduate studies because she unconsciously had equated succeeding and becoming a principal with "abandoning" her pupils in prison!

Here was another hidden conflict that had surfaced and had been robbing her of the mental energy she required to teach and study. Now she was able to resolve this problem which had been contributing to her mental depression.

Ms. Turner was under the impression that she had been "indifferent" when her fiancé, with whom she lived, had sexual relations with others as well as herself. Now she probed her real feelings about this. She found that she was, "very hurt, and I feel very insecure about him."

When she tried to work out a monogomous relationship with her fiancé, he broke the engagement. Ms. Turner felt that this was preferable to her failure to live with the many sexual affairs which he persisted in pursuing.

Presently, she is planning to be married in the near future. The man she is marrying is monogomous, a precondition she finds is necessary for her to be conflict-free in this area.

The apparent lack of significant causes for Ms. Turner's "endogenous" mental depression was shown to be false. The causes were found and were dealt with.

Now that Ms. Turner no longer tends to deny to herself her real problems, she is in a mentally healthier state to avoid a future depression.

Edward Finley, at twenty-two, was a year older than his brother Dan. Mr. Finley, perplexed, asked us, "Why am I so mentally depressed, while my brother Dan is such a happy-go-lucky guy?"

He continued, "Didn't we come from the same parents? The same school? The same opportunities? Why *me*, why should I be the one to get mentally depressed?"

Mr. Finley is expressing the most frequent heart-broken cry of the clinically mentally depressed, "Why *me*, aren't I the same as the others? Yet *they* don't become mentally depressed. Isn't the environment and the problems the same for me as the others? Yet why do *I* come down with mental depression?"

Mr. Finley learned in therapy that he *is* different from those who don't get mental depressions. Mr. Finley has had *different* girl friends from those of his brother. Dan's teachers, friends, experiences, boys clubs, church groups, and hobbies were *different* from his older brother's. Even his parents have *different* responses to their eldest son and their youngest one.

Edward Finley's attitudes, mind sets, and how he perceives life *do* differ from those of his brother. He brings different strengths and weaknesses to the same problems that confront his brother. Even the *number* of problems confronting each will be different. Obviously, the less successfully one handles problems, the more they will pile up on him.

There are always concrete reasons why some people succumb to a mental depression, while others do not.

Frequently, mental depression is a survival shield—but at what a price!

Tom Ward is a social worker who came to us for treatment for his mental depression.

Twice he had been mugged while trying to visit clients in their slum neighborhood. Mr. Ward's job didn't require that he risk his life by entering his clients' garbage-strewn, unlit slum stairs and halls. But Mr. Ward felt his conscience required he personally hand-deliver emergency rent and food checks to his needy clients.

Often the aged clients would become ill waiting to see

Mr. Ward in his tiny office. He would feel obliged to drive them home and help them up to their room. He would run a gauntlet of drug addicts, muggers, alcoholics, and sadistic sociopaths. The slum building he'd find himself in would often be in an area with the highest crime rate.

After escorting the sick client up to his room, Mr. Ward, heart pounding furiously in fear, would dash back to his car. Sometimes the tires would have been removed, windows broken, and his battery stolen.

Mr. Ward was courting mugging, serious assault, and, possibly, violent death. Yet he felt his conscience warranted his suicidal behavior.

When Mr. Ward became mentally depressed, he found he was having so much difficulty holding on to his job *that he was unable to visit or escort sick clients to their slum dwellings.*

Now Mr. Ward understands the psychodynamics behind his illness. His mental depression had developed *in the service of protecting his life!* The termination of his depression was helped to occur with this insight.

It is vital to recognize that clearing up one single important maladaptive behavior for Mr. Ward (or other patients) does not end a depression. There are other important maladjustments which the depressive suffers from. These must be diagnosed and treated. When the cluster of maladjusted behavior patterns are corrected by realistic actions by the patient, the termination of the depression is substantially assured.

This correction of a *group* of maladjusted behavior patterns need not take a long time. For just as the developing of one maladaptive type of behavior *brings on additional ones*—the extinction of one maladaptive behavior pattern helps *more speedily to erase other maladaptive behavior.*

A triggering of Mr. Ward's depression was his *continuous* fear of inviting the dangers encountered in slum buildings in economically depressed areas. He suffered what is known as "Old Sergeant Syndrome." Years ago, "Old Sergeant Syndrome" was called "shell shock." This occurred because very few soldiers can mentally tolerate a *continuous* period of active combat. If this condition extends without the relief of frequent leaves from the active front every few weeks, most soldiers develop a clinical mental depression.

These clinically depressed soldiers are not malingering. Their symptoms of helplessness are genuine. This is their unconscious defense to survive the otherwise extended period of facing death in the front lines.

In civilian life, the slum visits by Mr. Ward were his continuous "battlefield." Other depressed patients may have variants on the continuous "battlefield." It may be the reckless visits by naive women to the apartments of strange men, met for the first time at a social gathering. These thoughtless visits may invite rape and/or death. Actions that regularly jeopardize life may help induce clinical mental depressions. These self-endangering actions must be avoided—or the results may be a mental depression summoned to save one's life and limb.

The *conscious insights* developed by the patient to terminate present mental depressions are vital also for the prevention of *future* depressions.

GREAT EXPECTATIONS EQUAL GREAT DISASTERS

OUR FRIEND, "MR. SMITH," WAS PLANNING TO RETIRE from his executive position in a publishing company. He had been with them for thirty years. He'd just become 65.

Mr. Smith had booked a Mediterranean cruise to celebrate his retirement. He was to be paid a high, five-figure severance pay on retirement. He also owned considerable stock in the publishing company that was paying high dividends annually.

One month before his resignation became effective, he was examined and diagnosed as possibly having cancer. After a second consultation confirmed this, he was told to enter the hospital immediately for exploratory surgery. He entered the hospital as prescribed.

He did have cancer, which was removed. By the time he was back on his feet again, his retirement period had already begun.

His severance pay was not given to him. During his illness and recovery, his boss had liquidated the publishing company. Mr. Smith is in litigation with his former boss regarding his severance pay and his share of the now-liquidated business.

Mr. Smith remained emotionally stable throughout his ordeal. He was able to reconcile himself, not only of the losses of these vital monies, but also to his long-dreamed-of cruise to the sunny, historical cradle of western civilization.

How did he do it? What kept his emotional stability on its even keel? What kept him from even indicating the severe strain to which he was subject after these blows to his personal and financial survival?

One of the keys to his psychological survival is that Mr. Smith *was careful to maintain his expectations on a realistic level.*

It's not just that Mr. Smith knows that serious illness may strike at any time; nor is it just that he knows that financial security may vanish through a hundred causes. It is that he knows that *these things can happen to him too.*

Mr. Smith had *deliberately* discussed with friends the possibilities that any one factor vital to his survival *may go down* as well as up. His discussions served to *desensitize* him adequately when the double blow struck him.

Certainly, Mr. Smith has been severely hurt by these serious attacks on his health and income. But he is not reeling in dismayed surprise. He continues to work hard at not allowing himself to be caught in a vulnerable posture of improbable expectations.

He ribs us, "One of the reasons you shrinks haven't got me is that I'm not surprised when I meet up with hard knocks. They're in the cards. Who can be immune from them?"

He soberly reflects, a wry smile is flashed. "Sure, those beatings hurt, when they hit me. But can you imagine how much more painful they would be if I ignored the fact that setbacks are part of being alive?"

Since Mr. Smith's expected to suffer *some* severe blows

as part of his day-to-day living, he doesn't waste time being sullen when the blows come. Instead, he faces each setback courageously, and his realistic approach to life has helped him to avoid any attacks of clinical depression.

Everybody, now and then, must check with a competent psychotherapist to determine whether their lifestyle is on a survival path. You already know that you must have periodic checkups for your medical and dental health— before possible disease can gain headway. The therapist will check you objectively to see whether you're adequately protecting your physical health, your dignity, your solvency —and your view of reality.

The therapist will have time to warn you of stress areas that may be more than you can cope with. Tactics to dispose of or reorganize these dangerous stresses will be developed and acted on.

We find that many things happen to people despite their personal efforts to achieve or avoid these things. Only a part of their lives is under their absolute control; *and this control requires working at night and day*! Tragically, too many people are not taking care of the part of their life they could control. Can you imagine the helplessness these people foster by neglecting to control what they can of their lives?

Now and then, nice things happen to one—simply out of the blue. They were not earned, they just happily happened. During *most of one's life* this does *not* happen. Most of the time, vital but random happenings to you are negative, harmful—*unless you're in there protecting yourself*!

If we were to picture the world we all live in, it would be this:

All humans are in a giant boxing ring. Each of us is wearing boxing gloves and a fighter's attire. At birth, we are immediately sent to the middle of the ring. The bell instantly rings—the fight's on.

Some of us learn to keep our gloves up. The able fighters remain alert at all times, for blows are being rained on us from *all* directions.

The tougher scrappers learn to swivel their heads in all directions to anticipate and fend off the multi-blows. Therapists, also inside the ring, shout warnings to their patients.

The boxing match ends only when the boxers ultimately die naturally, are killed in the ring—or take their own lives.

Some survivalists in the ring help this period of continuous struggle to become a noble, glorious, and, frequently, humorous adventure. For most it is essentially a hazardous, rough journey. And for some, it's a nightmare, unparalleled even in the imagination of the most skilled writer of horror stories.

Keep your gloves up! For the killings are constant. Your survival is best insured by your *unceasing* vigilance. The blows will rarely cease being thrown at you.

One sure way to know you are alive is through this shower of blows! Only the dead don't get hit.

One can't afford combinations of blows to the jaw. We can tolerate one or two severe, jolting blows. Three or more, one after the other to the chin, often fells one. Many stagger to their feet after going down. But remember, there are no counts when you are floored. There are no Marquis of Queensbury rules of fair combat. Many hit below the belt, gouge eyes, rabbit punch, and gang up behind your back. They stomp you when you're down. No quarter is generally given. Rarely is mercy shown.

As a result, one of every ten people in the United States are in mental institutions—at least once during their lives. There would be more, but there are no beds for them.

Four of every ten in medical hospital beds are as severely mentally disturbed as those in mental institutions. One million of life's losers are in prisons. The boxing ring of life has a long list of knockouts.

As therapists, our work is to effectively, through behavioral and social science, keep as many of our patients on their feet in the ring as possible.

We would be delighted if the world would cease operating in a way analogous to a boxing ring. There are a number of ideologies that could convert the boxing ring to a more humane place in which to conduct the business of life. But no ideology in the past or the present has managed this. We cannot predict the future. Meanwhile, back in the boxing ring, we'll help the fighters to *defend* themselves. We advocate "neither a killer nor a victim be."

Each person in this ring must protect himself first. Then he can protect his loved ones, his family, his friends, and his society.

Everyone encounters grave difficulties in protecting themselves. All are hurting, the able are in pain only part of the time. All are bleeding—but at different rates. Some have time in the ring to smile encouragingly at others, while ducking blows at their own heads. Many snarl at each other; the blows they are absorbing seem beyond human endurance.

Tremendous stress situations occur frequently to everyone. You see it all around you in the boxing arena of life. Don't deny that the stress situations are real, and a threat—above all to yourself.

If you deny to yourself that the attacks are being mounted against *you*, you will not do anything to defend yourself or prevent them. This is a sure way to help bring on a clinical mental depression; and when it hits you—

you're the most surprised. You tell yourself helplessly, "I hurt badly, what's happened to me?"

Your denial to react, both emotionally and actively against the serious problems of everyday living has blinded you to your role as a stationary target. You don't even know what is hitting you! And you certainly are resisting the prevention of the slaughter; or counterattacking the stress situations.

In this dangerous state of self-delusion, the depressed person may instead attempt unconsciously to create reasons for the symptoms of his or her clinical depression.

Overwhelming fatigue is a symptom of depression. But rather than get at its original causes, the depressives may place themselves in an environment that must cause fatigue. So they work 18 hours a day, sleep two or three hours a night, then say, "Aha! If I didn't have to work so hard, then I wouldn't always be so tired!"

Frequently the family is blamed for the loss of energy of the depressed. They are accused to being too noisy, whether they're three or seventy-three. The accusations by the depressed are endless, and sometimes groundless. The depressed parent is unable to perform his or her key service for the children.

Parents are their children's fight managers in the boxing ring of life. They must also shield their children from the more lethal blows flung at them. The continuous attacks against the children, produced by life, generate great hostility in the children. The children may then strike at the people closest to them—their parents. It's a circular war in this ring, and the depressed parent tires more quickly from the blows thrown by both family and strangers.

As allies, we shout these encouraging strategies to you, as you're being battered in the big ring. These anti-depression strategies we offer you will help substantially to keep you unbowed, though bloody.

As it is so true of so many aspects of living, we must introduce here further paradoxes, contradictions, and ambiguities regarding *self-protection*. If we are exclusively concerned with self-protection, do we move inexorably in the direction of building our own isolated atom bomb shelters? Think of the price when one moves into one.

It is obvious that *to grow, and develop independence*, we must separate ourselves from the protection of parents. When we go to school, leave home, establish our own identities—these acts involve risks. Some of the risks are real, others less real. But to be our own person, we have to "give up" the illusory utopia of the completely safe way to live in the world.

At the same time, in the very service of surviving by growing, self-protection has a vital place.

Is it any wonder each of us must tread a swaying tightrope of both self-protection *and* reaching out to grow! Those who can't manage this precarious trip fall off by the hundreds of millions all over the world. Fortunately for human survival, most manage to climb back on the tightrope. Up there, again, they continuously balance these two forces necessary for survival.

PART THREE

REMOVING
THE SHAME FROM
MENTAL
DEPRESSION

NOBODY
CAN BLAME THE
MENTALLY DEPRESSED
FOR "MALINGERING"

THE SUFFERERS FROM CLINICAL MENTAL DEPRESSION CAN relieve their emotional agony somewhat by recognizing that it is *legitimate* to have tremendous coping problems as part of the depressed condition. The sufferers should feel no guilt or shame for their considerably less productive day than they formerly were accustomed to. Just as pneumonia patients shouldn't expect to carry on as before the onset of the illness, so must the mental depression sufferer accept lower levels of performance.

Just as no guilt is attached to coming down with pneumonia, so no guilt should be attached to suffering from mental depression. *This is the most important point about mental depression.* The sufferers must recognize that they should no more feel responsible for having gotten their mental depression than a patient who came down with pneumonia. This truth can save a torrent of anguish for sufferers from mental depression.

A long overdue emancipation movement for sufferers from mental depression is the organizing of *Mental Depression Anonymous.* Its goal, among other things, is *to educate*

*its members and society to recognize that, during a period
of mental depression, sufferers must not be looked down
upon* because they're not their former more vigorous selves.

There are 50 million Americans with subclinical depression, and 20 million suffering clinical mental depression. Their vast numbers could very successfully develop a
self-help organization. Therapists could be utilized to work
for this long-overdue organization. They would expedite its
function of helping terminate mental depressions as well as
helping to prevent their occurrence.

Just as some males have an overblown "macho" ego,
so is it with the mental depressives, who expect that a mental depression can't slow them down. The male with the
overblown masculine ego will fight at the drop of a hat to
prove his courage. So too, the mentally depressed must
avoid the trap of trying to prove to themselves that their
depressed condition is not affecting their behavior.

Mental depression *does* affect its victims' behavior.
Just as pneumonia victims don't bluster out the illness, but
use medical treatment to cure it, so must similar curative
actions be taken by mental depressives. Denial of the
ravages of mental depression to themselves is as harmful as
denying the dangerous effects of untreated pneumonia.

This does not mean the sufferer goes around announc-
ing his or her mental depressive state. It does mean the
sufferer doesn't deny to himself the slowing-down effects of
mental depression. This recognition helps the sufferer to
avoid feeling guilty and ashamed that he or she is not performing better. When the sufferer and the world understand
this, the agony of mental depression won't have the additional burden of demands for greater achievement on the
part of the already-struggling victim.

The mentally depressed sufferer is usually realistically

concerned about the cost of, and length of time spent in, therapy. A therapist can work out with the patient a 10- or 12-session program. Antidepressant drugs will be administered simultaneously.

An even lower-cost therapy program can result when therapy is group-administered.

Another significant advantage in group therapy is the lessening of the isolation symptom commonly felt by the depressive. Many problems and possible solutions will emerge which are common to the mentally depressed people comprising the group.

The patient may find that this brief therapy program is not sufficient. The therapist may then work out a realistic treatment program based on knowledge of the resources available and the patient's case history. For those for whom this brief treatment suffices, well and good. Even if the patient who requires longer therapy drops out, his or her brief treatment will have provided considerably more insight into causes and treatment of the depression than the patient was aware of prior to the treatment.

This brief treatment was most useful for Janice Brown, aged 36, a legal secretary. She had a very rigid, inflexible personality. She was suffering from mental depression. The following account illustrates a deeply embedded characteristic of her behavior.

One of her bosses asked her not to be a perfectionist in her typing. He told her it cut down her productivity. For months, Ms. Brown ignored his request. She felt she *must* type letters without a single erasure.

Finally, her job was threatened. From rigidity, Ms. Brown went to total compliance. Regardless of how sloppy the letters looked, she turned out considerably more than any other secretary in the law firm. This, too, was unacceptable to her employers.

In therapy she modified this character structure. She ceased to be totally rigid or totally compliant. She tailored her response to the specific situation, rather than making preconceived, stereotyped responses. She began to *test* the success of her defenses when she came into conflict with others.

She now finds that she's able to keep jobs longer—as well as friends. Her former character disorders of aggression, obsessiveness, and compulsion no longer plague her in key areas, and no longer contribute to depress her.

Jack Stanton, 30, a rising magazine editor, came to us in a clinical mental depression. He, his wife, and three youngsters were living with his widowed mother-in-law. He told us about his mother-in-law; that she was a fine woman, very ambitious for Jack and his family. Jack said he was very fond of his mother-in-law. She was pooling with him half of a down payment on a mortgage for a private home. There they planned to live together.

However, Mr. Stanton was worried this plan may not materialize because he had become so mentally depressed that he had requested and gotten a leave from his job. His mother-in-law, meanwhile, was not too quietly saying within his hearing that he was "crazy" and also lazy—that he was probably planning to desert his wife and children . . . and her.

"The worst part of this," Mr. Stanton said, "is that I don't know why I've mentally become so like a jellyfish. I have a loving family, a good job, I'm healthy, so is my family. Why has my mind become so—so—moronic? Why do I feel so totally inadequate, so helpless?

"I guess my mother-in-law is right, I'm just no good."

In therapy, Mr. Stanton discovered he had lacked the assertiveness to reveal that he never wanted his family and himself living with his mother-in-law. She was a very strong personality and had, in the short time they lived together in an apartment, made him and his wife "children" again. She was making their key decisions, and they were vying for her approval just as they had when they were youngsters, living under their parents' roof.

Instead of dealing with this reality, Mr. Stanton had repressed this truth. He turned his anger at this state of affairs inward, against himself. And he had not known he was doing this.

He eventually overcame this fear of letting others know what he legitimately felt was right. He competently cleared the air with his mother-in-law. He moved into the private home with his wife and children. His mother-in-law remained in the apartment Mr. Stanton previously shared with her. His depression began lifting. A few months later it had disappeared.

The above case does not mean that a family living with in-laws for an extended period of time is a negative living arrangement. It does mean that Mr. Stanton should never have accepted a mother figure to live with him in his own home. When he had failed to recognize this reality, the cover-up of his true feelings helped trigger a clinical mental depression.

Mr. Stanton now knows how to constructively ventilate his feelings without necessarily rupturing relations with others. Now he no longer feels false guilts when he raises *necessary* truths—even though it may cause discomfort before the air is cleared.

On discharge, Mr. Stanton told us, "I felt unburdened talking to you about my problems. Even if I hadn't rid myself of my depression, the relief of opening up about it would have helped me stop thinking that suicide is the only way out."

With Mr. Stanton, as well as other patients, we've also helped them discharge their pent-up rage through sublimation. They've taken up pursuits in the arts, sciences, social sciences, etc. By our patients' achieving these new abilities, instead of engaging in destructive acts, recovery comes closer.

Sue Benton, 20, a college senior, saw people as either all good, or all bad. Rather than recognizing that people are complex mixtures of plusses and minuses, they all had to fit Ms. Benton's stereotype of them.

Ms. Benton, who lived with her mother, sometimes felt that her mother was rejecting and frustrating her and was a "bad" mother. But this raised anxieties that Ms. Benton had never successfully worked out while growing up.

Her earlier good experiences had not been sufficient for her to tolerate her mother being "bad" sometimes. The effort to maintain a "good" mother image at *all* times and in *most* situations helped cause Ms. Benton's depression.

As Ms. Benton's insight increased in therapy, she stopped manipulating her mind to stereotype people; and in her relations with others she stopped unconsciously manipulating them to live up to her stereotypes of them.

For the first time, Ms. Benton began to see people as they really are. She gave up her defense as seeing them as "100 percent good" or "100 percent bad." She no longer demanded unconsciously, "Why aren't people more like me?"

Ms. Benton is now able to live with people who may be responsible for both good acts and bad acts. She no longer feels she has to abandon people when they do something "bad." And since she can tolerate it, she now feels that even when she erroneously commits a "bad" act, she won't automatically be abandoned by others.

Ms. Benton has expanded her narrow view to permit seeing the whole person. She can now respond to them more sophisticatedly, rather than in her former meagre, stereotyped manner of thinking and feeling.

Lorrain Stein, 48, did not attend her nursing class's reunion dance. Shortly afterward, she came for therapy for her clinical mental depression. She disclosed that she had avoided the nurses' reunion because she feared other nurses would pity her for neither being married nor having a steady male companion.

Ms. Stein was reflecting society's attitude of frowning on unmarried women. There is, actually, a cultural-social pressure on single women to find a mate. In addition to this ongoing pressure, Ms. Stein required tenderness and love which she was not receiving. Her free time was not spent in companionship and sociability; she was lonely, without someone with whom to share a close relationship. Her sexual needs were present and unfulfilled, though they diminished in the throes of her mental depression.

After a determined effort by Ms. Stein to satisfy these urgent needs, she found a companion with whom she developed a lasting relationship. Ms. Stein gave this relationship the same careful attention that she gave her job as director of nurses in a large municipal hospital. She had finally learned that a durable, ongoing relationship with a companion was a vital link in her network of defenses to fend off clinical mental depression.

Where a compatible love object is cultivated in one's life, the chance of an occurence of mental depression is lessened. And where mental depression does occur, despite the presence of a compatible love object, the depression's duration may be appreciably shortened.

During the mental depression, *the sufferer is prone to*

overreact to people and situations. David Lessing, as a youngster, resented when his family would fail to celebrate his birthday with a party and gifts. Often, his birthday would pass without his receiving a gift.

A bachelor of 30, Mr. Lessing and his father visited his married brother on Father's Day. (David Lessing lives with his widower father, from whom he never separated his dependency relationship.) Father and married son were given Father's Day gifts. David's father was given a number of gifts, including a deep green vase. David was not given any gift, as he was not a father.

As the Father's Day celebration broke up David said bitterly to his father in the presence of the celebrants, "If you take that green vase, Dad, I won't enter our apartment! The color of that vase is evil!"

Efforts were made to reason with David, to no avail. Ultimately the vase was left in the married brother's home.

In the therapy session, David at first told us he felt an evil spell existed in the green vase. As he began to discuss it, he said, "Well, nobody gave me even one gift, and all the guys present were given a couple. Then only a few of my relatives even talked to me at the party. I felt left out of everything. It was the same as when I was a little kid and my family skipped my birthdays. I felt that all I amount to is a failure. Then when all the fathers were taking home their gifts, I suddenly got very angry. So I blurted out that green vase is evil. I see I was really saying that everybody slighted me just because I wasn't a father and because I'm a failure."

Like other depressives, Mr. Lessing tends to overreact to both fancied as well as real slights. His family, friends, co-workers, employers, and neighbors are suspected of negative motives when generally there is no such intention.

Daily occurrences that do not irritate the non-depressed frequently cause the depressed to overreact. It is important that the depressed recognize their tendency to overreact and take greater care in their responses to those acts triggering their reactions. Mr. Lessing, for example, found that "loud" chirping birds were disturbing his sleep. As Mr. Lessing became increasingly aware of the real causes for his depression and eliminated them, he was no longer disturbed while sleeping.

Mr. Lessing developed the ability to take in his stride rejection by others, sharp criticism by others, exclusion from a group, and the missing of a goal. He no longer attributed major importance to every commonplace irritant.

As Mr. Lessing matured, he exercised his democratic right not to be required to know everything immediately—or yesterday.

He also no longer reacts to stress situations in a preconditioned, automatic way. He neutralizes his former reflex responses by allowing time to think through a better response to the problem. He's given up many anachronistic responses from old experiences that are no longer relevant.

As a small child, he was frightened by adults. As an adult, Mr. Lessing carried along his early feelings that he was still helpless, while other adults were exaggeratedly powerful. He has learned to monitor his reactions to the anachronistic, helpless feelings. Mr. Lessing gives himself a moment now to put together a response that is appropriate to the here and now.

As Mr. Lessing is hit with a specific stress, he no longer overreacts automatically. He sets up an analysis of the stress instead of creating an emotional storm over it. He tries to solve the stress, and also prevent it from happening again. It's a vastly different response from that which he used to demonstrate. Now he puts up a *wall of thinking the problem through* between the problem and his response. Overreaction is now more easily kept inside a realistic response framework.

As a fall in self-esteem helps trigger depression, it is vital one doesn't undertake impossible tasks or vast numbers of projects. These both generally ensure failure, with a corresponding drop in self-esteem. Ms. Geraldine Holmes came to us with this serious problem, among others.

Ms. Holmes is head nurse in a drug addiction ward. Her patients are hard, tough, and full of "street smarts."

Ms. Holmes was struggling to finish her master's in social work, in evening courses. In addition, she was the organizer and moving spirit of a large feminist organization.

Now she felt that she wasn't performing adequately in any of these roles, as she felt herself to be "moronic, guilty of failure, and I have no moral fibre to snap myself out of my depression."

She has since reduced her work-load and responsibilities to a realistic level. With her judicious selection of work projects, more efficiency has resulted. Her self-esteem has been fully restored. She is no longer mentally depressed.

The state of "well-being" is a useful bulwark against mental depression. Well-being includes some financial security, self-esteem, good health, bodily vigor through exercise, acceptance of one's appearance, compatible love relations, etc. The more of these positive factors you have operating in your life, the stronger the protection against mental depression.

CHAPTER
XII

"HOW COME YOU'RE NOT AS SUCCESSFUL AS JACK?"

BOB GAINES, AGED 44, IS ASKED BY HIS WIFE, "HOW COME you're not successful like Jack?"

Suffering from a clinical mental depression, Mr. Gaines mournfully tells us he agrees with his wife, "After all, I have the same education as Jack, I'm as smart, as good looking as he is, yet he's got a quarter of a million in the bank!"

Mr. Gaines and his wife watch TV commercials. Every family in the U.S. is shown on the tube as beautiful, happy, and owning everything from a huge color TV to a new luxury appointed auto. All are flying to "exotic" parts of the globe in jets. *By comparison*, the Gaineses are "failures."

Mr. Gaines tells us, "If I can't save at least $10,000 in the bank, I'm in trouble." He doesn't have it in the bank.

When Mr. Gaines sets up $10,000 as his minimum bank account, he's set himself up to be a loser. For, until he acquires that set sum, he's branded himself as inadequate. All of these self-defeating acts are due to setting goals in one's head that are tied to self-images of inadequacy if they are not achieved.

Goals can and should be planned for—but there's no useful purpose served in attributing failure to oneself if they are not accomplished.

Mr. Gaines justifies his placing his self-esteem on the line to achieve $10,000 in the bank. He calls it "survival money." After he *reconsiders* what survival means, he boils it down to "If I'm not harrassed as I go through life—maybe that's survival. After all, I don't stand on a welfare line to receive a pittance to pay for food, clothing, and shelter. I don't have to go, hat in hand, to anyone to tide me over the weekly and monthly bills."

In therapy, Mr. Gaines examines what damage he does to himself by comparing himself to others. He reflects that if somebody has $100,000 in the bank, any comparison of himself to the other must put him down. There's always somebody with more strength than he, more wit then he, more culture than he, more looks than he, more hair than he. If somebody sings better than he, must he shrink in a corner at that party because he's "inferior" by comparison?

Mr. Gaines has been destroying his self-esteem by continuously measuring himself against others. There is no limit to this self-defeating battle, self-administered. He may be helped in this invidious comparison game by self-styled concerned people who may be found as close as one's spouse and friends of long standing.

While Mr. Gaines has been shooting himself down inside, he's been hindered from shooting down the many real stresses attacking him on the outside.

Mr. Gaines has ended the comparison suicide sweepstakes. He now sees himself as a unique individual—rather than a measuring rod against the Rockefellers and Robert Redford.

Some comparison of ourselves with others is inevitable. As we are going to do some anyway, let's examine how to do it right. We know the wrong way is how depressives destructively do it. The right way is *doing something constructive* in the area in which we are making comparisons.

Now Mr. Gaines understands that "all men are *not* born equal." The U.S. Constitution states that all men are created equal—meaning that all people are *equally entitled* to their Constitutional rights. That's all.

Everyone is equal. Yet in the present world, some are just more equal than others. This occurs through superior biological, neurological, social, and economic inheritance.

Nobody is ever born exactly equal, not even identical twins! Even *their* personalities vary.

The ruler of the ancient world, King Alexander of Greece, visited the philosopher Diogenes. Alexander offered Diogenes anything he may request. Diogenes genially requested Alexander to move aside and not block the sunlight.

Diogenes was too wise to compare himself *seriously* with Alexander. In that path lies mental depression. Alexander, were he wise, would not have naively compared his philosophical ability to that of Diogenes.

CHAPTER

XIII

_____

**PSYCHOLOGICAL HEALTH
IS DEPENDENT
ON THE FREEDOM
TO MAKE CHANGES**

ALL HUMANS WHO ARE SUCCESSFUL IN AVOIDING MENTAL depression help achieve this by avoiding routine lives. They are constantly seeking new answers and approaches to the changing times.

They eat varied menus. They see a variety of movies, plays, concerts, and television shows. Books, magazines, newspapers, and radio programs that offer new viewpoints are examined. Vacations in different places are planned. For *variety* is the foe of neurosis—which is automatic repetition.

Variety is not only the spice of life—it *is* life. This is why prison life is so deadly, and why most prisoners develop mental depressions. Prisoners are not free to make changes, or exercise freedom of choice.

Throughout life we are prone to forget about the freedom of making choices or changes. We regain this trait after we become sufficiently bored. Sometimes we wait until we've become dangerously mentally depressed before we utilize the freedom to make changes in our lifestyle.

The important task to work at is to make changes *before* we reach pathologically depressed levels. This does not mean that all routines are wrong. It is functional to routinize brushing your teeth. The same goes for having the water and oil checked in a car.

As Dr. Lawrence S. Kubie puts it, "Indeed, much routine is essential for the survival of the human being and/or race. If we did not repeat breathing automatically, eating or drinking, and many other things in a routine way, we could not survive."

This type of routine is most essential and useful. But there is nothing more deadly than the boredom suffered when you relate to someone whose every response is predictable. The strongest symptom in mental depression is the feeling of boredom by the patient—and the patient's overwhelming fear he is a bore to others. This accounts for the typical withdrawal by the patient from the company of others—the terror of being so boring that others will think that the depressive is mentally retarded.

Irrational self-protection carried to an absurdity will become "perfect safety." But no growth develops, and eventually boredom results.

Perhaps the obsessive person (often called stiff or humorless) unconsciously or consciously makes a contract with God: "Let me live safely and I'll deny myself any pleasure." This may be a piece of our Judaic-Christian work ethic.

Repetitive thinking results in obsessive and compulsive behavior. It induces automatic, stereotyped thinking. The antidote to this danger are plans and actions to develop new attitudes and varied activities.

It has recently been found in studies of depressed life-styles that depressives don't involve themselves in as many "fun" activities as the non-depressed. By deliberately seeking out varied activities, as against routinized, automatic ones, we help to reduce depressed states.

CHAPTER

XIV

KNOWING THE *EFFECTS* OF DEPRESSION, YOU ARE IN CONTROL

JOAN BENTON, 19, CAME TO US DURING HER DEPRESSION. One of her strongest symptoms was her feeling that she must debase herself. One of the ways she abuses herself is her belief that she had committed unforgivable sins.

Ms. Benton is a college student. Among her "sins" is her deep guilt about requesting her teenage sister to play her records very low while she's studying for her college exams. Joan further debases herself, after passing an exam well, by considering herself accidentally lucky that she passed. Her self-image (public or private) as a student, is one of being "stupid and a failure." Before she became mentally depressed she had considered herself to be a fairly able student.

Ms. Benton developed the insight that some of mental depression's byproducts are self-debasement, and the conviction that one has committed unforgivable sins. Sometimes the above by-products are so strong that they are almost delusional.

Now she recognizes that these distortions are due to her depression. She *cognitively recognizes* that she is neither slow-witted nor sinful. *Emotionally*, though, the *feeling* persists that she is slow-witted and sinful. But she is in some control; she realistically recognizes now that, though her mind is not as able as before her depression, she can make it work better now until her depression is eliminated. As for her sinning, she says, "I *know* I'm not sinning—even though I feel I am, when I'm not really!"

*   *   *

Dr. Freud analyzes the causes of depression as the result of a lost love object, a serious loss, or a separation. The depressive's anger and/or hate of the loss of the love object unconsciously manifests itself by self-accusation. The ego and the lost love object have become identified *as one* by the sufferer. In order to punish the lost love object (now incorporated in the ego) the victim develops a loss of self-esteem. Freud showed that the unconscious hostility of the depressive *turns inward.*

E. Bibring examines this loss of self-esteem in the depressive. He sees it as due to the collapse of the ego in the sufferer. The ego collapses because it aspired too highly— to be loved and valued; to be strong and secure; to be loving and good.

The depressive simply demanded more from reality than what he believed he was getting. Even getting *some* love, or getting to be valued *somewhat* is a tall order in this real world of strife. It is not easy always to be strong and secure. "Secure" is a state that shifts constantly by the thousands of conflicts inside and outside the person. Financially, to be "secure" is something neither our government nor the largest corporation can guarantee, by always operating on a profit margin; and any virus in the environment can topple our "secure" state of health.

As for aspiring to be continuously "loving" and "good," that requires sainthood, free of trial and temptations, a condition which doesn't exist in the real world. These rigid, unreal standards that are self-imposed by the depressives—and sometimes by outside perfectionists—must be lightened if the depressive is to recover.

The above type of failure or loss of perspective turns it into a problem—and the problem may snowball into a mental illness. Often the patients grew up in an atmosphere in which any bad feelings expressed by them were condemned as reflecting on the parents or society. This open expression of bad feelings or discontent angers the older group. The children associate this anger with rejection of themselves by those in power.

Consequently, these repressed children can only express this bad feeling when they are made to look "legitimate"—when these bad feelings emerge as *caused by mental depression.*

Survivalists *learn* to live with some unachieved aspirations. Survivalists learn to tolerate some unrealized goals, some knotty conflicts, some frustrations, some lessening of self-esteem, some self-reproach, some disappointments, some erosion of self-confidence, some stress, some tensions, some worries, and some lack of gratification. This reality learning prevents their succumbing readily to mental depression and its resulting helplessness.

Psychiatrist Arnold Beck finds depressed patients suffer "paralysis of the will." They fall prey to this because they consider that most of their acts will have a negative outcome. But when the patients are persuaded that *they can succeed*, they will be more prone to pursue the act. The depressives will help themselves by *carefully examining their chances of succeeding in an endeavor.* This realistic approach will help end their paralysis of the will.

Dr. Beck discovered that when therapist, family, or friends encourage the patient to initiate an activity, retardation of mind and subjective fatigue of the patients are reduced.

Lichtenberg and Beck find that when the depressed patients succeed in an activity, their level of aspirations, their mood, and their expectations of success, all rise higher. Success breeds success in depressives as well as non-depressives.

There are three triggers that may significantly bring on a mental depression:

1. The death of a person important to the patient (his or her mate, child, parent, friend, etc.).
2. The recognition by the patient that an important relationship has failed (one with his or her mate, parent, friend, boss, business partner, significant associates in a voluntary organization, etc.).
3. A strong disappointment in work or ideology to which the patient has devoted his or her life (career, politics, religion, etc.).

The key to avoiding these triggers is to develop as much control over them as possible.

In the instance of losing one's job, it is rare not to be severely affected by it. Loss of a job is a frequent trigger to mental depression. Dr. Malzberg finds that the economic depression of the Thirties was very visible in the depressives' stresses. In 1933, 26.2 percent of first-admissions patients diagnosed as depressive psychotics were shown to have as the precipitating factor loss of employment or financial loss.

Today, a study of the U.S. public by pollster Yabilinsky discloses that the majority of people are not prepared psychologically for the loss of their jobs. His conclusion is that large numbers of them will be triggered into a mental depression should they lose their jobs.

It is obvious that unless society deals effectively with large-scale unemployment, great sums of tax money will go into the treatment of the unemployed depressives and their dependents.

The above three triggers that bring on depression demonstrate the danger of making exclusively a person, movement, or career the be-all and end-all. By becoming flexible, one can select more alternatives when any or all of these significant three fail.

PART FOUR

TERMINATING A MENTAL DEPRESSION

CHAPTER
XV

THE GREATEST VALUE
IN LIFE
IS *YOUR LIFE!*

WHEN THE PATIENT, THE THERAPIST AND THE FAMILY OB-
serve that suicide by the depressive is a *real* possibility,
hospitalization should be agreed on until this stage of the
condition is terminated. Drug therapy reduces the suicide
risk. Lithium works well with the manic phase of a depression.

Electric shock therapy works quickly to terminate
many severe depression conditions. Sometimes only a few
shock treatments are needed for a temporary recovery from
depression. Psychotherapy and drug therapy can then
complete the treatment as well as prevent future depression
attacks.

Neither electric shock treatment nor drug therapy can
fundamentally change the depressive personality. The basic
problems that caused the depression have not been dealt
with. Electric shock treatment essentially permits the patient to bury temporarily the basic problems that caused the
depression.

Drug therapy helps the patient be less sensitive to depression or pathological elation. But the possibility of the

depression's returning remains as long as the basic problems that caused it still remain. Only efficient psychotherapy can remove the causes of mental depression.

Dr. Silvano Arieti finds a "dominant other" (the spouse, business firm, an ideological movement one belongs to) in depressives' lives that may trigger depressions. This occurs when the patients find the dominant other is no longer nurturing them with approval, love, guidance, or hope. The dominant other also "fails" the patients by dying or being seen in another light.

When the patient is found to be predominantly self-blaming, his or her dominant other figure is found by Dr. Arieti often to be perfectionist, ultramoralistic, or possessing obsessive-compulsive attitudes. The dominant other unintentionally increases the patient's feelings of guilt by declaring, "For many years I took care of you; now you take care of me."

Dr. Arieti, with the patient's permission, discusses with the dominant other environmental changes and the relationship with the patient to relieve the patient of much of the unbearable yoke of guilt, unnecessary responsibility, lack of accomplishment, and losses.

Then the patient works out with Dr. Arieti the clarification of how to live *for himself*. Prior to treatment, the patient had not known how to live for himself. He had not been listening to himself. He had not been asserting himself. All the patient cared about was to win the approval, love, admiration, and care of the dominant other.

Care is exercised to develop insight in this patient regarding the extent that he invited control over himself by the dominant other. Recovery can't genuinely develop until the patient recognizes the part he played in creating this pattern of submissiveness. Then a new role by the patient is developed. The patient ends the role of the dominant other and converts the dominant other to a constructive "significant other."

Since women comprise over sixty percent of the depressed patients, we recognize afresh the damage our patriarchal society does in having women depend on dominant others. Sometimes dependent women, lacking insight, switch from male dominant others to female dominant others.

Women have a battle on two fronts. One is the fight against the patriarchal culture that conditions their dependency. The other is their own submissiveness to this patriarchal order.

CHAPTER

XVI

YOU MUST HAVE MENTAL DEPRESSION *TREATED*

No SOCIETY LIKES DEPRESSIVES. "LAUGH, AND THE WORLD laughs with you. Cry, and you cry alone."

Since ancient Biblical times and the Greek Classical Age the mentally depressed have suffered the same agonizing symptoms. And each age has rejected those in a mentally depressed condition. It is only relatively recently that society struck the chains off the mental patients incarcerated in houses of bedlam.

Dr. Howard P. Rome realistically says, "There is no overlooking the fact that, from time immemorial, there has been a well-established deep-rooted abhorrence of mental and emotional illness.

"It is an accretion of cultural beliefs—mythical thinking having to do with demonological possession and consequent loss of control.

"As a consequence, this generates an understandable fear and revulsion. Then too, because of what might be called the 'asylum tradition,' there is an associated stigma that appends to mental and emotional illness.

"This, to a greater or lesser degree, affects the patient,

his family and friends as well as the referring physician's attitudes, and therefore colors the entire referral process."

One thing follows from all this. Society must stop rejecting the mentally disturbed if it is to deal realistically with mental depression. This is not a luxury for society, it is a grim necessity. Any of us may become mentally depressed. Many already suffer this condition. And the large numbers who have overcome it want to prevent its recurrence.

Masked depressions are common in millions of patients. Alcoholics are depressives who try to self-medicate their depressions with liquor. It always fails to mask the depression—which thrives on this diet. Drug addicts also self-medicate their depression—their fate is the same as the alcoholics'; with police prosecution an added stress to their depression.

Gambling addiction is another mask for mental depression. The ultimate in extreme masking of a mental depression is the use of violence to hide the depression from oneself. This may vary from physical bullying to joining a violent gang or militaristic organization that glories in its professional death-dealing efficiency.

In depressed patients examined by Drs. Serry and Serry, symptoms that masked mental depression were:

central nervous system disturbances masked 25 percent of the patients;
gastrointestinal tract symptoms masked 22 percent of the patients;
general ill-health masked 20 percent of the patients;
musculoskeletal symptoms masked 11 percent of the patients;
cardiovascular complaints masked 10 percent of the patients;

genitourinary tract symptoms masked 5 percent of the
patients;
respiratory tract problems masked 3 percent of the patients;
skin problems masked 1 percent of the patients.

Severe headaches, with durations that are incapacitat-
ing, frequently mask the underlying depressive condition.
Irritability, fatigue, and hypersensitivity may be mistaken as
the effects of backaches or headaches. In reality, they may
be the signs of a mental depression.

Viral diseases, such as influenza, infectious hepatitis,
and infectious mononucleosis, frequently help trigger a
mental depression. For a while, the physical disease may be
considered to be causing the symptoms of depression: withdrawal from people, forgetfulness, preoccupation, mono-
syllabic response, slow speech, hesitation in doing things,
confusion, difficulty in remembering, reluctance to accept
responsibilities, and avoidance of decision-making. Eventually these may be found to be the result of a masked depression.

Patients may confuse the diagnosis of the examining
physician by physical complaints and symptoms. Intestinal
discomfort, dizziness, left chest pains, skipped heart beats—
all may mask the underlying cause, which is a mental depression. A thorough clinical and radiological laboratory examination will then fail to find that these symtoms occur
due to a physical cause.

When ulcers are corroborated by X-ray, or organic
heart disease is found, the psychological causes of depression that may also co-exist may be ignored or overlooked.

A thorough physical and psychological testing can
avoid a misdiagnosis. This includes a careful scrutiny of

shifts of mood of the patient in order to avoid overlooking a masked depression.

*   *   *

Dr. James M. A. Weiss finds that suicide rates tend to decrease in times of prosperity, and increase during times of economic depression.

Dr. J. Choron conservatively calculates that between 6 and 7 million U.S. residents have attempted suicide.

Drs. E. S. Paykel, J. K. Meyers, and J. J. Lindenthal carefully surveyed 720 of the general population of New Haven, Connecticut. They uncovered 32 suicide attempts for every completed suicide.

Dr. J. Weiss finds, "Sainsbury's investigations of persons who had committed suicide in England also demonstrated a psychiatric diagnosis of serious depressive illness in a large majority of cases. And reports from several major studies in the relationship between psychiatric disorders and ultimate death from suicide reveal that about 15 percent of persons found suffering from depressive illness will ultimately die by suicide. This compares to 1 percent of the general population."

Dr. J. Weiss' treatment to prevent suicide deals with the psychological, physiological, and sociological aspects of the person involved. The acute stresses in one or all of these areas must be relieved by psychotherapy, chemotherapy, and, where possible, by enlightened community service providing jobs, education, housing, medical care, etc.

These social measures and required medical care are vital. In addition, Dr. J. Weiss underscores the necessity for the depressed suicidal patients to receive psychotherapy. This is the surest way the depressive can understand and deal with the "need" for suicide.

In those instances where the patient, the family, and the therapist agree on hospitalization, a therapeutic milieu is the best type of hospital. There, as in most psychiatric hospitals today, the staff doesn't automatically remove the depressed patient's belt, tie, shoelaces, and safety razor. Nor do they remove other objects thought to be usable in suicide attempts, unless otherwise indicated.

The present, humanized policies utilize the "therapeutic community" and the "open door" for patients. Judgment is exercised regarding these measures where patients are a present danger to themselves.

Suicide rates went down in mental hospitals when these measures replaced the rigid, robotlike, automatic repression of free movement of depressed patients. By eliminating isolation, alienation, and dependency in the mental hospital, depressed patients terminated their depressions more rapidly.

Increased training, sensitivity, and knowledge in hospital personnel is decreasing the suicide rate in hospitals. Hot lines (emergency telephone anti-suicide centers) now make available instant psychological help to depressed sufferers who are potentially suicidal.

To those advocates of the "right" of a person to take his or her own life, it must be pointed out that suicide is a *symptom*. It is a symptom of biological, psychological, and cultural causes that the suicidal person *has little understanding of*. Suicide is a disorder, not a free moral choice. If free choice existed here, who would choose a killer role—and of their own self?

Dr. Freud cut through the myth of the "right" to commit suicide. He said, "The moment one inquires about the *meaning* or *value* of life, one is sick since objectively neither 'meaning' nor 'value' have any existence."

Everyone who can must participate in saving the de-pressed from suicide, particularly since nine out of ten re-cover from the depressed condition. This is work for the social activist, the good friend, the devoted relative, re-searchers of depressed behavior, the public health specialist —and the depressed person.

We are frequently asked by our patients for the an-swers to the heart-rending question, "What's the point in my living? The way the world looks, it won't get better for me. I don't have the strength left to try to overcome all the problems in life. I'm worthless, anyhow. Even when I'm employed, the job adds up to meaningless work, anyway."

Two vital points are raised by the patients here. One is: "What satisfaction can I get out of this tough world?" The other is: "What use am I to anybody in this world?"

Depressed persons *can* get *some* satisfaction out of life —as long as they recognize that they have to *fight* for it *as everybody else must do.* Life is a *battlefield,* with peace of mind won at rare intervals only. The patient must stop be-lieving that most people have a lot of money, a great car, a beautiful house, and are beautiful people who are living it up.

It is also not true that most people are respected, ad-mired, and loved by all. People, for the most part, are en-gaged in the same desperate battle for money, respect, power, material goods, health, good spirits, love, friendship, etc.

Many depressed patients ask, "What's the importance of being alive?"

"What contributions will I ever make to this world?"

"What good am I?"

The depressed patient must recognize that these questions don't have *easy answers*. They never were able to be answered simply. Since time began for humans, philosophers have been pondering what it's all about. And much time has been spent trying to decide what contributions are worthwhile for people to make.

There may be, ultimately, answers to the questions about the importance of being alive, or the contributions one should make. But depressed persons are too full of guilt and low self-esteem to even consider them. In their depressed condition, they are their own harshest critics. Therefore, they are not in a good position to answer realistically why it's important to be alive, or what contributions can be made to life.

The depressed persons are wise to hold off trying answer these questions, and it's helpful to take a moratorium on them. When their depression is terminated, they can then work out answers to these questions. When the depressed persons consciously believe they *must* answer these questions during their depression, they may allow themselves to become obsessed with them. It's like having a temperature of 105 degrees and persisting in measuring how strong, how independent, and how alert one is!

During the interim of the depression, the last person to judge the value of being alive or making a contribution to humanity is the depressed person. The best answer here is to take a rain check on the final answers in these areas. We do not denounce the victims, the mentally depressed. We do describe the powerful task they are forced to engage in.

One's general physician may not always refer a mental depressive to a psychotherapist. Some general practitioners are not comfortable in this role of referral—others fail to see that their patient is depressed and that his symptoms are being masked by physical illness. The tests in this book provide patients with an opportunity to know whether they are masking their true condition with hypochondriasis.

After determining that one *does* have a mental depression, a psychotherapist should be seen as soon as possible.

CHAPTER

XVII

STRENGTHEN YOUR "LIFE WISH" OVER YOUR "DEATH WISH"

Dr. Freud discovered that humans are continually engaged in two opposite types of activity. One group of activities keeps the human being alive. The other group of activities hastens the death of that same individual.

He found that the set of acts that keep the human surviving includes: eating balanced meals, getting sufficient sleep and rest, realistically exercising the body, neither neglecting or overdoing work and play, maintaining a satisfying social life, and fulfilling sexual needs.

The life-seeking type of person recognizes, as Freud did, that a sound mind can best exist in a sound body.

Destructive death wishes are generated in the minds of those who ignore the above laws of survival.

Freud called those with healthy behavior "Eros" seekers (lovers of life). The self-destructive types were termed by Freud "Thanatos" seekers (pursuers of death).

Freud enlightened the world regarding the roles of masochists (self-punishers) and sadists (unwarranted punishers of others). Both belong equally to the Thanatos camp —inviting death, rather than life. Both the masochist and the sadist deny to themselves that this is their goal. They repress this recognition. It, nevertheless, surfaces in free-floating anxiety, guilt, rage, indecisiveness, and hostility to others.

A married couple, our patients, unwittingly revealed to us their unconscious self-abuse:

Ms. Wagner is a fifty-year-old lawyer. She went on a Caribbean cruise with her husband, an architect who is also in his fifties. They travelled first class. They had been assured by their travel agent of excellent service by the cruise ship's personnel.

On the first night at sea, Ms. Wagner rang for her steward at midnight. She ordered a gourmet dish which the ship's information packet said was available. The steward denied it was in the larder.

Ms. Wagner had a fierce argument with the steward. When he maintained his position in a disagreeable manner, she reported him to his superior officer. Mutually hostile vibrations were given off by Ms. Wagner and the steward. Reluctantly, the steward served her the demanded delicacy, complaining that he had been forced to give her what was really not available to other passengers.

The following afternoon, Ms. Wagner played deck tennis with a middle-aged black woman, Ms. Henry, who occupied the next cabin. A rapid shipboard camaraderie was established. Ms. Wagner confided to her neighbor how irritated she had been over their mutual steward's unco-operativeness, saying, "After all, at the rates we're paying —I certainly have the right to expect better food than I have ordinarily in my refrigerator at home!"

Ms. Henry listened sympathetically.

"How are you doing with the steward? Has he given you a hard time too?" Ms. Wagner inquired.

"Well, yes and no," Ms. Henry explained. "When I

rang for him late last night, he eventually showed up in about a half an hour. Then I knew I'd better look out for the curve he might throw me.

"When I ordered lobster and avocado salad, he told me they were out of it.

"So I put on my most appealing smile and said to the steward, 'My husband and I really had looked forward to the late snacks on board ship that we rarely enjoy at home. It would make our trip if we could live in such luxury.

" 'But I suppose it's too much to hope for. After all, you do have so many demands on these delicacies. It's no wonder you've run out of them. So anything that's left would be fine. We can't have everything in life, can we?'

"The steward returned in a few minutes with two over-flowing platters of what we had originally ordered—and a real good bottle of wine. He said he had gone to the chef who permitted him to get it from his own stock.

"I suppose the steward works better when he's jollied a bit. I don't always win when I run into this type. But I experiment a bit, until I can work out some relationship where a difficult type finds it embarrassing to his own conscience if he resists cooperating.

"When all fails, I can always report him to the one above him."

In the therapy session Ms. Wagner smiled as she concluded what took place on the cruise. "For the rest of the trip I did it Ms. Henry's way. Where it failed, I tried other methods. It worked like a charm with our steward, from whom we parted on the best of terms."

Ms. Wagner chose *life* when she gave up her unsatisfying method of dealing with the steward, and selected an option more rewarding to her. A masochist clings to nonfunctional methods to relate to another person.

Ms. Wagner needed another experience to develop the "Eros" approach to making life pleasant for herself.

She developed greater insight into "Eros" behavior in the following incident which she told us about. "I visited a close friend who lives in a cooperative high rise building on Manhattan's west side.

"Every time I parked my car in that building's minimal charge parking lot, I'd get dirty looks and growls from the older man and a teenager who are employed there.

"The way in which the parking lot is operated is that the drivers do their own parking, lock the doors, and hold onto the car keys. They do the same when removing their car. The parking lot employees at no time do anything but collect the parking fee. So I failed to see why these two attendants were so rude and surly toward me.

"I told my friend, during one of my visits, the irritation I felt about the rudeness of the parking lot attendants.

"She laughed and explained, 'Why don't you try giving them a tip? It would, I guarantee, turn them into living dolls.' "

Ms. Wagner ruefully observed, "I tip them now. The tip means nothing to my budget—but now when I park, butter would melt in their mouths, those attendants are so warm.

"I see I had originally felt the tip was unnecessary, because the attendants never handled my car. But for the small tip now, I've made it pleasant for myself—and that's what life is mostly all about. You only pass once through life, why not choose to make it as pleasant a trip as possible for oneself?"

The week after Christmas Ms. Wagner told us of an incident that demonstrated she had begun to choose Eros over Thanatos. She informed us, "I frequently work after hours at the law firm. A cleaning woman, quite assertive, cleans our offices after working hours.

"I can tell that she feels inconvenienced because I work late nearly every evening. She can come into my office only after I leave, which causes her to interrupt her work on another section of the floor.

"I can't help inconveniencing her—I've got to work at my own pace to hold my job, too. This has been going on for several years.

"But this Christmas, I had learned something from the cruise and the parking lot incidents. I gave this annoyed office cleaning lady a Christmas gift of a sum of money.

"Now, when this cleaning lady sees me, she greets me like an old friend. It's made life after hours at the office much more relaxing than before.

"You know, if I continue to make life more pleasant for myself—I really will enjoy living longer."

It requires examination when irritating situations keep repeating themselves. A lover of Eros will attempt to figure out how to remove the repetitive assault on their emotions. A Thanatos-type will masochistically reassure themselves of the "rightness" of their dysfunctional actions—and permit stresses to build up to a possible trigger for a mental depression.

CHAPTER
XVIII

ILLUSIONS
OF UNLIMITED CHOICES
BRING GUILT

SALLY ELLENDER, AGED 33, FELT GREAT GUILT BECAUSE she resigned from her social worker's job. She lamented that she had let down her clients who needed her help. Prior to Ms. Ellender's employment as a social worker, she was a very competent fashion designer for a prestigious high fashion house.

Because Ms. Ellender was clinically depressed, she found it too difficult to remember the many details required to service her clients' many pressing needs. Her collaboration with her colleagues in psychiatry, psychology, medicine, nursing, and pharmacy had deteriorated as well.

Rather than being able to accept that her depressed condition was real and genuinely made her social work duties considerably more difficult, she guiltily felt she was "indulging" herself improperly by her lessened efficiency.

Because she functioned with considerably less stress as a fashion designer, Ms. Ellender gave up her social work and got a job in her former field.

After Ms. Ellender was in psychotherapy, she lost her guilt about leaving social work due to mental depression.

She had gained insight that her mental depression was *real*. She accepted that mental depression *does reduce job efficiency*. She now saw that she had not let her former clients down. Rather, she recognized that she had a right to work at any job that met her needs during her mental depression.

Had she come into therapy earlier, while holding her social worker job, she would have been helped to hold onto it—if that had been what she wanted. In treatment she would have relinquished the guilt and weighed whether the extra pressure of holding the social work job would have best met her needs.

In any event, therapy would have offered her more options regarding holding either of her two skilled jobs. Above all, *she would not have had the illusion that during a mental depression one has the same identical choices regarding holding jobs* as when one is not depressed.

The considerable guilt she felt because of this illusion would have been eliminated. This would have allowed more rapid elimination of the depressed mood, thinking, and behavior.

For those many millions in this country who are no longer youthful, middle-age depression may develop due to the social factors oppressing the chronologically "mature."

Sam Goldsmith, 51, found that at this age jobs were harder to obtain. Physically, he feels somewhat more tired after work than when he was younger. Unlike older chairmen of the boards, M.D.s, and judges, Mr. Goldsmith's job skills earn less as he enters middle age and beyond.

In therapy, the clinically depressed Mr. Goldsmith gave up the illusion that he has *personally failed* because his earning power has diminished. His economic expectations and self-blame are now more realistic.

Alicia Grayson, aged 47, is suffering from middle-age

depression. She's past menopause and feels "over the hill." She no longer has children at home to rear. She feels useless. Although she doesn't have as many options in life as when she was in her twenties, she observes some of her peers enjoying activities and functioning well. Rather than feel guilty that she's a "failure," she should work out with a psychotherapist a program to function as well as some of her peers.

Due to modern medical breakthroughs, most people today are alive in their mid-fifties. They are around and wonder how they'll manage—what roles they are to play. This has contributed to make this era different from those preceding it. In Freud's generation—the 1890's—the psychopathology was hysteria and anxiety neuroses. After World War II, it was the era of character disorders. Today, our forms of psychopathology are more conspicuous; we live in the age of clinical mental depression.

Over 20,000,000* of our population suffer the agony of clinical mental depression. This grim fact helps to keep the depressed from feeling they are uniquely isolated with a rare mental condition. Feelings of isolation enlarge the terror of feeling boxed in; separated from the rest. Knowing that 20,000,000 more are in a state of clinical mental depression makes the sufferer feel less "crazy."

To use this knowledge *effectively*, the sufferer from mental depression must go on and say, "O.K., there are 20,000,000 more people depressed like me—but *I'm not going to remain in that state of agony with them*!

"And I'm not going to attribute the wrong causes for my mental depression. For that will only delay the ending of my depression."

---

* 50,000 more are victims of a subclinical depression.

CHAPTER

XIX

**FOR THOSE WHO
HAVE
MENTAL DEPRESSION
BUT CAN'T
AFFORD
PSYCHOTHERAPY**

PSYCHOTHERAPY IS ESSENTIAL TO TERMINATE MENTAL DE-pression quickly. Psychotherapy also helps develop the insight necessary to avoid the mental depression's recurrence.

Many self-defeating excuses are invented by sufferers of mental depression to resist psychotherapeutic treatment. Certainly it is true that seeking psychotherapeutic treatment with no money is no walk in a rose garden. But the advantages in seeking psychotherapy are immeasurably worth the difficulties incurred.

There are three sources of psychotherapeutic treatment available without cost:

1. Government-supplied psychotherapists;
2. Non-profit agencies that provide psychotherapists;
3. Some private-practice psychotherapists who accept Medicaid or Medicare patients. (Unemployment, or old age makes one eligible for either plan.)

This is survival we're talking about—psychotherapy is essential for the mentally depressed. There is nothing disgraceful in receiving free psychotherapy, as there is nothing improper in receiving free medical care for a pneumonia patient unable to pay for the treatment. For those who can't afford psychotherapy, the free treatment of their mind is their inalienable right.

CHAPTER

XX

THE LAST LINE
TO REMEMBER
REGARDING
MENTAL DEPRESSION

HOW WILL THE PSYCHOTHERAPY OFFERED HERE ENSURE more rapid termination of clinical mental depression? *When one acts as prescribed here.* Then, and only then, can this psychotherapy appreciably hasten the end of clinical mental depression.

This is the *most vital part of the treatment* for mental depression. This book offers the depressed *specific things to do* that more speedily terminate, or prevent the recurrence of, mental depression.

This is *not* mainly an *insight* book, assuming that by understanding alone one can magically terminate, and prevent the recurrence of, mental depression.

Here is the "iceberg" that we've discovered that *shows humans successfully battling* against mental depression:

THE HUMAN THINKING PROCESS:

10% OF THE SUCCESSFUL DEFENSE AGAINST MENTAL DEPRESSION IS: **INSIGHT** ON THE CAUSES, CURES AND PREVENTION OF MENTAL DEPRESSION

90% OF THE SUCCESSFUL DEFENSE AGAINST MENTAL DEPRESSION IS: INSIGHTFUL **ACTIONS** TAKEN TO TERMINATE OR TO PREVENT RECURRENCE OF MENTAL DEPRESSION

This book offers treatment and prevention of mental depression for the *individual.* In a following book, the authors will disclose their investigations of *society's* responsibilities to *prevent* the epidemics of clinical mental depression and subclinical depressions now sweeping all countries.

The tragic reality is that hundreds of millions of people are suffering the agonies of mental depression—while the rest of the population is constantly in danger of falling victim to this dread condition.

EPILOGUE

WHAT YOU CAN DO
TO COMBAT
MENTAL DEPRESSION
FOR YOUR
OWN PERSONAL
AND
NATIONAL BENEFIT

SEVENTY MILLION PEOPLE SUFFERING FROM MENTAL DE-pression in the United States is a powerful group to combat mental depression. Their relatives and friends are their natural allies in the battle to end mental depression.

Together, this makes those opposed to the agonizing effects of mental depression well over half the population of the United States. This group has a personal stake in ending mental depression, which is the number one killer among mental illnesses. Because mental depression seriously reduces the productivity of 70,000,000 Americans, it is a national disaster.

Crisis intervention by the government to help rescue this one-third of a nation in the grip of mental depression is most urgent. The Bill of Rights declares that this group of sufferers also have the inalienable right to the pursuit of happiness.

As a first step, the government should legislate funds for a national organization, Mental Depression Anonymous. This coast-to-coast organization may be based on some of the self-help member cooperation principles that

Alcoholics Anonymous developed. However, members of Mental Depression Anonymous will not publicly divulge their personal problems in open meetings. This would only be done in privacy with the trained psychotherapists who will staff Mental Depression Anonymous. Both the members and the psychotherapists will democratically operate Mental Depression Anonymous.

The following Associated Press dispatch* reports that this category of mental health proposal can be forwarded to the President's Mental Health Commission:

> Mrs. Carter said that she had the following goal in mental health as First Lady: "For every person who needs mental health care to be able to receive it close to his home, and to remove the stigma from mental health care so people will be free to talk about it and seek help. It's been taboo for so long to admit you had a mental health problem."
>
> As honorary chairman of the President's mental health commission, she said that she planned to travel around the country to meet with professionals in the field, the parents of mentally afflicted children and possibly patients.
>
> "If we can get them all working together for the same goals, then we can draw up legislative proposals to give to Jimmy so he can get them implemented for us," she said.

An essential reason why the country needs this proposed government funded Mental Depression Anonymous organization was summed up by one of our patients, "I'm a single woman. I need to save some of my salary in case I get ill and am unable to work for a sizable period of time. Yet, if I have to pay $35 to $50 for an average therapy session —I won't be able to save money for a financial emergency."

* *The New York Times*, New York, March 10, 1977.

This patient earns an executive's salary, yet she finds it impossible to pay her living costs, therapy costs, and still save money. Far too many in our society earn considerably less than she does. Mental Depression Anonymous can be a start in meeting the need for effective, professional mental therapy at little or no cost.

You readers, your relatives and friends may support this program to end mental depression by writing to:

The President's Mental Health Commission
Washington, D.C.

I support the legislative proposal for a government funded Mental Depression Anonymous national organization. Staffed by trained psychotherapists, it will be democratically administered by members and staff psychotherapists. Its emphasis will include mutual self-help by the members. It is a matter of life and death that the 70,000,000 American victims of this debilitating, and often lethal illness return to normal functioning through the implementation of this legislative proposal.

Very sincerely,

Name . . . .

Address . . . .

PART FIVE

10 DAILY PROGRESS REPORTS EXERCISES TO HELP TERMINATE MENTAL DEPRESSION

VERY IMPORTANT

To derive maximum benefits in filling out these *Daily Progress Reports*, the following should be kept in mind:

The purpose of filling out the *Daily Progress Reports* is to aid your coping abilities. It is *not* to test yourself in order to find out whether you are failing in the activities covered. You are not in this world to be put on trial. You are not here to be measured to establish whether you are a success or failure.

Neither you nor anyone does you a service by demanding from you more than you're able to achieve at any given moment.

It is not pathological when you don't score a ☑ today. A lot of us can't score daily.

It is not unusual if you didn't succeed today. What's wrong with trying and not achieving? *The important thing is you survived today.* That's much more than deceased achievers can say.

If you didn't score today, remind yourself of the youngster all of us knew in school—the one who got 95 percent in his exam, yet felt miserable because he hadn't scored 100 percent.

If you didn't score today while dealing with life, you have the *right to be mentally unclear* in life's situations. Life is difficult, and so you didn't manage to score easily. All of us have the right to be indecisive. Nobody knows how to succeed without making mistakes. That's why they put erasers on pencils.

The right to be honestly wrong is as much our right as the right to life, liberty, and the pursuit of happiness.

If all 10 of your *Daily Progress Reports* each day showed you won on each of them, that would be most unusual.

Often, events occur over which we have no control, or we were not exercising vigilance, or we lacked experience in those particular situations. We must allow for some failure, or a great deal of it—as the situation calls for.

Although Leo Durocher's credo "nice guys finish last" is not a realistic plan to follow, there is a word of warning in Mr. Durocher's statement. It is telling us that eternal vigilance is the price we must pay to get through each day.

In our culture, winning in every situation seems to be our only acceptable lifestyle. This perfect-score obsession is not a reality principle. Life characteristically means "you win some, you lose some."

Consider yourself unique in the population when you are able, on any single day, to fill out *all* the Daily Progress Reports with a ☑.

"HELPING OTHERS" THERAPY IMPROVES ONE'S *OWN* PSYCHE

1- After editor Robert Latham recovered from a stroke, his speech, thinking and memory were impaired. He then volunteered to work with retarded children . . .

2- . . . and found that his own injured mental abilities improved as he helped the retarded youngsters develop their skills . . . he has since trained and become a competent psychotherapist.

REVIEW WHAT YOU'VE DONE TODAY TO HELP SOMEONE:

– Become more independent
– Better able to cope with a problem
– Learn something useful
– Do anything that made life a little better for them . . .

. . . CHECK ONE BOX A DAY WHENEVER YOU HELPED SOMEONE MANAGE:

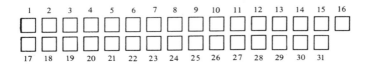

1	2	3	4	5	6	7	8	9	10	11	12	13	14	15	16
☐	☐	☐	☐	☐	☐	☐	☐	☐	☐	☐	☐	☐	☐	☐	☐
☐	☐	☐	☐	☐	☐	☐	☐	☐	☐	☐	☐	☐	☐	☐	
17	18	19	20	21	22	23	24	25	26	27	28	29	30	31	

"ASSERTION" THERAPY THAT PREVENTS *DESTRUCTIVE* COMPROMISES

1- Jim Dirken is a capable science writer . . .

2- . . . who was given a severe reprimand by his recently hired supervisor. The new supervisor asserted that the cause for reprimanding him was that Mr. Dirken *stutters* . . .

3- . . . this made Mr. Dirken carefully observe his new supervisor's overall supervisory procedures. Mr. Dirken found that the new supervisor's supervision techniques regularly used destructive attacks on those under him. Mr. Dirken promptly looked for another job, as the new supervisor had too many connections on the job to be successfully confronted. Mr. Dirken found a new job and resigned . . .

. . . CHECK ONE BOX A DAY WHENEVER YOU CONSTRUCTIVELY CONFRONTED A PUTDOWN—OR WHERE IT MADE MORE SENSE TO REMOVE YOURSELF FROM THE ABUSIVE SITUATION:

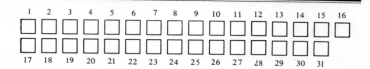

1	2	3	4	5	6	7	8	9	10	11	12	13	14	15	16
17	18	19	20	21	22	23	24	25	26	27	28	29	30	31	

DON'T PERMIT ANY PERSON OR SITUATION TO TOTALLY DETERMINE YOUR WELL-BEING

1- Ann Jensen was deeply in love with an apparently mature man. When her lover left her for another, **Ms.** Jensen felt so unwanted and shattered, that she wished she were dead . . .

2- . . . in therapy, Ms. Jensen developed insight into **why** she felt so totally alone after her lover left her. It **was** due to her *depending on* another person as her **measure** of her desirability to all others . . .

3- She stopped her helpless dependency on another **person** to measure her worth or her happiness. She found **others** *did* enjoy her company, despite her lover **having** given her up. Ms. Jensen later married another **man** whom she loved. She resolved that neither her **husband** nor anyone else exclusively held her happiness in *their* hands . . .

. . . CHECK ONE BOX A DAY, WHEN YOU FIND YOU DON'T DEPEND *TOTALLY* ON A LOVER, RELATIVE, FRIEND, SUPERVISOR, JOB, OR SITUATION FOR YOUR EMOTIONAL WELL-BEING:

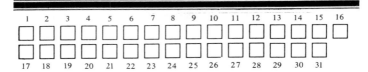

1	2	3	4	5	6	7	8	9	10	11	12	13	14	15	16
□	□	□	□	□	□	□	□	□	□	□	□	□	□	□	□
□	□	□	□	□	□	□	□	□	□	□	□	□	□	□	
17	18	19	20	21	22	23	24	25	26	27	28	29	30	31	

IV / DAILY PROGRESS REPORT

STOP GAMBLING WITH YOUR LIFE BY BURNING YOUR BRIDGES BEHIND YOU

1- Louise Weston was very bored with her job as secretary in a magazine publishing company. She felt there was no future for her in that company. She felt her degree in journalism was wasted on this job . . .

2- . . . she resigned her job—*even though she had not found another job first.* She had mistakenly believed it is too hard to look for another job, while still employed. She could have used her vacation to go on the job hunt. She might have also scheduled some interviews after five o'clock. Sure it's not easy—but most worthwhile goals are hard to come by, (unfortunately) . . .

3- . . . since Ms. Weston had a very small bank account, in a few weeks she had to try to get welfare—or accept another job that was inferior to the one from which she had resigned. She settled, optionless, on a job at a lesser level . . .

. . . CHECK ONE BOX WHEN YOU WORKED OUT A SAFE EXIT FROM A DIFFICULT SITUATION—INSTEAD OF PAINTING YOURSELF INTO A CORNER:

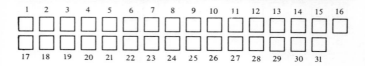

END DEPENDENCE ON EXPECTATIONS THAT ARE UNREALISTIC

1- Ms. Grace Garment wrote extremely superior soap operas for the TV serial *Edge of Night*. She demanded from herself such a high degree of quality for each script she wrote—that they bordered on perfection. Even her TV producer stated that Ms. Garment expected perfection from herself, far beyond the level required for her scripts. This helped trigger her mental depression . . .

2- . . . when a person is obsessed with the idea that every undertaking must result in perfection, a psychotherapist's technique is to ask "How high is up?" Then follow it with the plan to set limits. In therapy one learns to give up unrealistic expectations. For example, workoholics tend to lose their job perspective. They drive themselves, and their co-workers, to achieve the *impossible*. The ultimate result of this unrealistic expectation is loss of self-esteem by the perfectionist and those who allow themselves to be victimized by the perfectionistic individual . . .

3- – Did *you* avoid demanding excessively more quality work than is being produced by competent people in the field?
   – Did you diplomatically bring to your superior's attention his excessive job demands, that unrealistically exceed the quality or quantity of work that performance on the job requires?
   – Did you eliminate from your *behavior* any other unrealistic expectation that you are aware is impossible to occur?

. . . CHECK A BOX EACH DAY WHEN YOU WERE ABLE TO AVOID AN UNREALISTIC DEMAND:

1	2	3	4	5	6	7	8	9	10	11	12	13	14	15	16
☐	☐	☐	☐	☐	☐	☐	☐	☐	☐	☐	☐	☐	☐	☐	☐

17	18	19	20	21	22	23	24	25	26	27	28	29	30	31
☐	☐	☐	☐	☐	☐	☐	☐	☐	☐	☐	☐	☐	☐	☐

A *SOUND* BODY IS ABLE TO MORE EFFECTIVELY HOUSE A *SOUND* MIND

1- James Franklin's mental depression had left him feeling continuously physically weak and tired. We advised him to do daily physical exercises, because he sat at a desk most of the day. He went to a bookstore and checked some books on exercises done in the home. He selected a structured exercise routine that he felt most comfortable with . . .

2- . . . after exercising a few weeks, to the accompaniment of cheerful music, Mr. Franklin felt his body was in a state of vigor and power. He was now eating balanced meals, and reduced to a healthy and attractive weight . . .

3- . . . short of an emergency, Mr. Franklin went to bed *before* midnight, regularly. His exercises, balanced meals, anti-depressant medication, and reading in bed to induce sleep, rewarded him with good results. He began to enjoy refreshing sleep, and awakened without his former fatigue which he suffered from constantly. Physically feeling well—Mr. Frankin was able to concentrate on his emotional and fiscal problems in an energetic fashion. The termination of his mental depression was speeded up by his developing a sound body . . .

. . . CHECK A BOX IF YOU: –ATE A BALANCED MEAL(S) –DID SOME EXERCISES (PREFERABLY THOSE IN A BOOK ON EXERCISES AND PHYSICAL FITNESS) –GOT TO BED BEFORE MIDNIGHT

SPEAK POSITIVELY OF YOURSELF TO OTHERS. DON'T KNOCK YOURSELF TO OTHERS— THIS HELPS DEVELOP SELF-ESTEEM

1- Arlene Lustig found she was jeopardizing her job by frequently telling her supervisor of her minor errors, and confessing that she was unworthy of holding her job. Ms. Lustig did the same with her fiancé. She re-cited to him her minor deficits, so that he began to hesi-tate about going through with the marriage. All these self-attacks lowered her self-esteem. With a constant pattern of self-deprecation, mental depression nearly always follows. Ms. Lustig came to us with a clinical mental depression. . . .

2- . . . in therapy, she learned not to disclose her real or imagined weaknesses to anyone in sight. She ruefully observed, "Nobody has to put themselves down—there are enough hostile people around already doing it to those who allow snipers to attack them". . . .
. . . Ms. Lustig now talks about her strengths to others —modestly, but firmly. She does not hide her skills, resourcefulness, and competencies under the proverbial bushel. She neither boasts nor does she indulge in self-deprecation. But she made an inventory of her abilities, and keeps that up front . . .

3- – I didn't put myself down today. (At least not as much as I used to in the past.)
– I pointed out to others a successful skill or action of mine, that would have otherwise gone unnoticed.
– Since I didn't expect to be perfect today—therefore I didn't call attention to the human mistakes I made.
– The only weakness or error I brought to another's attention was necessary to report—to prevent serious consequences if it was kept hidden.

. . . CHECK IF YOU DID ANY OF THE ABOVE TODAY TO RAISE YOUR SELF-ESTEEM:

1	2	3	4	5	6	7	8	9	10	11	12	13	14	15	16
17	18	19	20	21	22	23	24	25	26	27	28	29	30	31	

EVERYBODY HAS THESE THREE INALIENABLE RIGHTS FOR THEIR ENTIRE LIVES

1- *FIRST RIGHT* – Our patient, Charles Lurie, was deprived of these rights in the past. Today, he has internalized these rights and declares: "I'm not supposed to know everything. Therefore, I won't feel inadequate when I am faced with issues I didn't know about. If they are really necessary to my relationships with people, or to hold my job—I'll try to learn what I have to know . . .

2- *SECOND RIGHT* – "Learning about new things, that I find necessary to know, may take months. I have the right to take a reasonable amount of time to learn what's necessary . . .

3- *THIRD RIGHT* – "I have the right to be wrong, or make a mistake. (I don't deliberately exercise this inalienable right.) For those demanding or expecting flawless perfection from me—they should consort with angels . . ."

. . . CHECK IF YOU'VE DONE ANY OF THESE TODAY:

■ I DIDN'T KNOW SOMETHING TODAY—AND IT DIDN'T INJURE MY SELF-ESTEEM BY NOT KNOWING IT.
■ I MADE A MISTAKE(S) TODAY, PROVING SIMPLY THAT I'M NOT AN INFALLIBLE HUMAN BEING.
■ SOMETHING DEVELOPED TODAY THAT I BELIEVE I SHOULD LEARN MORE ABOUT. UNLESS IT'S AN EMERGENCY—I AM ENTITLED TO A REASONABLE TIME TO GET THE ANSWERS. IF I WAS UNDULY PUSHED REGARDING THIS—I POLITELY REQUESTED THE HUSTLER TO GET OFF MY BACK:

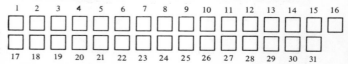

THE THREE ESSENTIAL ROLES IN LIFE THAT ALL MUST WORK HARD AT—IN ORDER TO HELP TERMINATE OR PREVENT MENTAL DEPRESSION

1- *Is my income adequate to pay my essential bills?*
If I'm untrained to make ends meet, I will enlist the aid of a job counselor, a social worker, or a psychotherapist. This may insure my skill at becoming economically independent.

2- *Is my social life adequate?*
If not, I'll tenaciously seek out cooperative friends to develop warm relationships.

3- *Is my love life a good one?*
If not, I'll unwaveringly seek an adequate partner with whom I can build companionship and a mature sexual life together. In the process to find or hold my partner, I'll further:
  – Develop interests, skills, values and ideals
  – Maintain a sound body, good grooming, attractive attire, and a pleasant environment

. . . CHECK WHAT YOU'VE DONE TODAY TO ACHIEVE THE THREE ESSENTIAL ROLES IN LIFE:

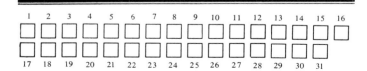

SURVIVAL DEPENDS ON LIVING ONE'S LIFE—NOT ALLOWING OTHERS TO LIVE YOUR LIFE

1- As a child, Carla Gomez was told by her parents that her high marks in school made them very proud of her. Carla mistakenly achieved high marks in school mainly for her parents' sake. She began living for them, instead of for herself.

2- As a teenager, Carla became overly concerned how her friends rated her. She began to live for her friends' approval, instead of *her own* views, values, opinions and judgments.

3- When Ms. Gomez became a schoolteacher, her principal's opinion of her became her guide whether she was competent or not. Ms. Gomez was still seeing life through eyes other than her own. Her husband, and later, her children—*they* decided for her whether she was a good wife, companion, mother, cook, driver, and budgeter. In Ms. Gomez's treatment for her mental depression, she learned to live *her own life*. This removed her helpless dependence on others. With power, came a rise in self-esteem—a vital factor in ending mental depression.

... CHECK IF YOU RATED YOUR OWN SELF TODAY, RATHER THAN ANOTHER DOING THIS VITAL SERVICE:

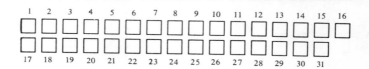

BIBLIOGRAPHY

Akiskal, H. and W. T. McKinney. "Depressive Disorders: Toward a Unified Hypothesis." *Science*, 182:20–29, 1973.

Arieti, S. "Affective Disorders: Manic-Depressive Psychoses and Psychotic Depressions: Manifest Symptomology, Psychodynamics, Sociological Factors, and Psychotherapy." *Amer. Handbook Psychiat.*, 2nd ed., Vol. 3, 449–90. New York: Basic Books, 1974.

————. *The Intrapsychic Self.* New York: Basic Books, 1967.

Ascher, E. "A Criticism of the Concept of Neurotic Depression." *Amer. J. Psychiat.*, 108:901–8, 1952.

Balinton, M. "New Beginning and the Paranoid and the Depressive Syndromes." *Int. J. Psychoanal.*, 33: 214–24, 1952.

Beck, A. T. "Depressive Neurosis." Silvano Arieti (Ed.) *Amer. Handbook of Psychiat.*, 2nd ed., Vol. 3, 61–90. New York: Basic Books, 1974.

————. *The Diagnosis and Management of Depression.* Philadelphia: University of Pennsylvania Press, 1973.

————. "Thinking and Depression: Idiosyncratic Content and Cognitive Distortions." *Arch. Gen. Psychiat.*, 9:324–33, 1963.

Bibring, E. "The Mechanism of Depression." P. Greenacre (Ed.), *Affective Disorders: A Psychoanalytic Contribution to Their Study*, 13–48. New York: International Universities Press, 1953.

Court, J. H. "Manic-Depressive Psychosis. An Alternative Conceptual Model." *Brit. J. Psychiat.*, 114:1523–30, 1968.

Durkheim, E. *Le Suicide.* New York: The Free Press, 1951.

Engel, G. L. "Anxiety and Depression-Withdrawal; The Primary Affects of Unpleasure." *Int. J. Psychoanal.*, 52:183–96, 1971.

Freud, S. *Group Psychology and the Analysis of the Ego.* Standard Edition, 18:69–43. London: Hogarth Press, (1921) 1955.

————. *Mourning and Melancholia*. Standard Edition, 14:243–58. London: Hogarth Press, (1917) 1957.

————. *On Narcissism*. Standard Edition, Vol. 14. London: Hogarth, 1917.

Friedman, A., B. Cowitz, H. W. Cohen, and S. C. Granick. "Syndromes and Themes of Psychotic Depression." *Arch. Gen. Psychiat.*, 9:540–9, 1963.

Goldfarb, A. I. "Masked Depression in the Old." *Amer. J. Psychother.*, 21:791–96, 1967.

Grunker, R. R., J. Miller, M. Sabshin, R. Nun, and J. C. Nunnally. *The Phenomena of Depressions*. New York: Hoeber, 1961.

Jones, R. O. "Depressive Reactions: Their Importance on Clinical Medicine." *Canad. M. A. J.*, 60:44–48, 1949.

Kay, D. W., J. R. Garside, J. R. Roy, and P. Beamish. " 'Endogenous' and 'Neurotic' Syndromes of Depression. A 5- to 7-Year Followup of 104 Cases." *Brit. J. Psychiat.*, 115:389–99, 1969.

Krains, S. H. *Mental Depressions and Their Treatment*. New York: Macmillan, 1957.

Kubie, L. S. "The Nature of the Neurotic Process." Silvano Arieti (Ed.) *Amer. Handbook Psychiat.*, 2nd ed., Vol. 3, 3–16. New York: Basic Books, 1974.

————. "The Relation of Psychotic Disorganization to the Neurotic Process." *PSA Assoc.*, 15:626–40, 1967.

Lehmann, H. E. "Psychiatric Concepts of Depression: Nomenclature and Classifications." *Canad. Psychiat. Assoc.*, 4 (Suppl.):1–12, 1959.

Lendrun, F. C. "A Thousand Cases of Attempted Suicide." *Amer. J. Psychiat.*, 115:389–99, 1969.

Lorand, S. "Adolescent Depression." *Int. J. Psychoanal.*, 48:53–60, 1967.

Mendels, J. "Electro-Convulsive Therapy and Depression: I. The Prognostic Significance of Clinical Factors." *Brit. J. Psychiat.*, III:675–81, 1965A.

————. "Electro-Convulsive Therapy and Depression: II. The

Significance of Endogenous and Reactive Syndromes." *Brit. J. Psychiat.*, III:682–86, 1965B.

————. "Electro-Convulsive Therapy and Depression: III. Method for Prognosis." *Brit. J. Psychiat.*, III:687–90, 1965C.

Paykel, E. S. "Classification of Depressed Patients: A Cluster Analysis Derived Grouping." *Brit. J. Psychiat.*, 118:275–88, 1971.

Poznanski, E. and J. P. Zrull. "Childhood Depression." *Arch. Gen. Psychiat.*, 23:8–15, 1970.

Rado, S. "Psychodynamics of Depression from the Etiologic Point of View." *Psychosom. Med.*, 13:51–55, 1951.

Resnick, H. L. P. (Ed.). *Suicidal Behaviors: Diagnosis and Management.* Boston: Little, Brown, 1968.

Rosenthal, S. H. "The Involutional Syndrome." *Amer. J. Psychiat.*, 124 (Suppl.):21–35, 1968.

Schmale, A. H. Jr. "Relationship of Separation and Depression to Disease." *Psychosom. Med.*, 20:259–77A, 1958.

Stengel, E. "Some Clinical Observations on Psychodynamic Relationships Between Depression and Obsessive-Compulsive Symptoms." *J. Ment. Sc.*, 94:650–52, 1948.

Walton, H. J. "Suicidal Behavior in Depressive Illness." *J. Ment. Sci.*, 104:884–91, 1958.

Weiss, J. M. A. "Suicide." Silvano Arieti (Ed.) *Amer. Handbook Psychiat.*, 2nd ed., Vol. 3, 743–65. New York: Basic Books, 1974.

Wold, C. I. "Characteristics of 26,000 Suicidal Prevention Center Patients." *Bullet. Suicidol.*, 6:24–34, 1970.

Wyatt, R., J. B. Portnoy, D. J. Kupfer, F. Snyder, and K. Engelman. "Resting Plasma Catecholamine Concentrations in Patients with Depression and Anxiety." *Arch. Gen. Psychiat.*, 24:65–70, 1971.

Zetzel, E. R. "The Depressive Position." In Phyllis Greenacre (Ed.), *Affective Disorders.* New York: Intl. Univ. Press, 1953.

INDEX

229

ABOUT THE AUTHORS

Psychotherapist Ms. RAY WEISS was educated at the Metropolitan School of Nursing in New York and at Marymount Manhattan College. She has completed graduate studies at C. W. Post Center of Long Island University and has studied group psychology and psychoanalysis at the Washington Square Institute of Mental Health and Psychotherapy in New York. She has been a practitioner in the psychiatric wards of Bellevue Hospital in New York City, and for seven years she was Co-Director of the Creative Workshop for Disturbed and Retarded Children of Nassau County, New York. She treats mentally depressed patients in family, group, and individual therapy. A frequent contributor to professional journals and speaker at professional seminars, she is presently with the Queens Hospital Center in New York.

Psychosocial-psychotherapist CARL WEISS received his B.A. in Psychology from Brooklyn College and did graduate work at Queens College and The New School for Social Research in New York. He studied psychoanalytic therapy at the National Psychological Association for Psychoanalysis, and studied psychotherapy with Dr. Hans Oppenheimer and child psychotherapy with Dr. Malcolm Marks. He has worked with the mentally depressed patients in the psychiatric wards of the Veterans Administration Hospital in Brooklyn, and for seven years was Co-Director of the Creative Workshop for Disturbed and Retarded Children of Nassau County, New York. He has also worked with disturbed adolescents in prison, and co-authored, with David James Friar, *Terror in the Prisons*. He is a frequent speaker on TV and radio on mental depression therapy.

DR. STEPHEN H. KEMPSTER, psychiatrist, has trained resident psychiatrists and psychologists at Einstein and Roosevelt Hospitals in New York. His extensive private practice consists mainly of depressed patients. Consultant Editor and author of the Introduction, Dr. Kempster's extensive experience in terminating mental depression makes this book invaluable.